FOR A BBQ MASTER

CONTENTS

INTRODUCTION — 7

RUBS AND MARINADES

All-Purpose BBQ Rub — 9

Sweet and Spicy Chicken Rub — 10

Rich Coffee Rub for Beef — 11

Lemon-Herb Rub for Lamb — 12

Citrus and Herb Marinade — 13

Soy and Ginger Marinade — 14

Spicy Yogurt Marinade — 15

Apple Cider Vinegar and Mustard Marinade — 16

MEAT RECIPES

BEEF ON THE GRILL

The Ultimate Grilled Burger — 18

Garlic Butter Ribeye Steak — 19

Herb-Crusted Beef Roast — 20

Texas-Style Brisket BBQ — 21

St. Louis Style Ribs — 22

Grilled Beef Cheeks — 23

CHICKEN AND TURKEY

Spiced Grilled Chicken Breast — 24

Honey-Sriracha Chicken Wings — 25

CONTENTS

BBQ Chicken Thighs — 26

Applewood Smoked Turkey — 27

Ultimate BBQ Turkey Delight — 28

Spicy Turkey Drumsticks — 29

PORK AND LAMB

BBQ Grilled Pulled Pork — 30

Herb-Marinated Pork Chops — 31

Sweet and Spicy Pork Ribs — 32

Minted Grilled Lamb Chops — 33

Rosemary and Garlic Leg of Lamb — 34

Rack of Lamb with Mustard Crust — 35

FISH AND SEAFOOD

Grilled Salmon with Lemon Herb Butter — 37

Mediterranean Grilled Tuna Steaks — 38

Cedar Planked Fish — 39

Fish Tacos with Mango Salsa — 40

Beer-Steamed Mussels — 41

Garlic Butter Shrimp Skewers — 42

Grilled Lobster with Herb Butter — 43

Seared Scallops with Balsamic Reduction — 44

Grilled Octopus with Olive Oil and Lemon — 45

Spicy Grilled Squid with Lemon Basil — 46

CONTENTS

Grilled Tuna Steaks with Avocado Salsa — 47

VEGETABLES

Grilled Asparagus with Lemon Zest — 49

Charred Corn on the Cob with Herb Butter — 50

Smokey Grilled Eggplant Slices — 51

Jalapeño Poppers Stuffed with Cream Cheese and Wrapped in Bacon — 52

Spiced Cauliflower Steaks — 53

Grilled Stuffed Bell Peppers — 54

SIDES

Classic Coleslaw — 56

Cheesy Grilled Garlic Bread — 57

Smokey Baba Ganoush — 58

Mexican Street Corn — 59

Italian Grilled Polenta — 60

Middle Eastern Tabbouleh — 61

DESSERTS

Grilled Pineapple with Cinnamon Honey Drizzle — 63

Grilled Pound Cake with Berry Compote — 64

Chocolate-Stuffed French Toast Skewers — 65

Texas-Style Smoked Brisket — 66

Grilled Banana Boats — 67

CONTENTS

Grilled Peach and Ricotta Parcels — 68

Grilled Honey-Mint Fruit Skewers — 69

CONCLUSION

Beyond the Embers — 70

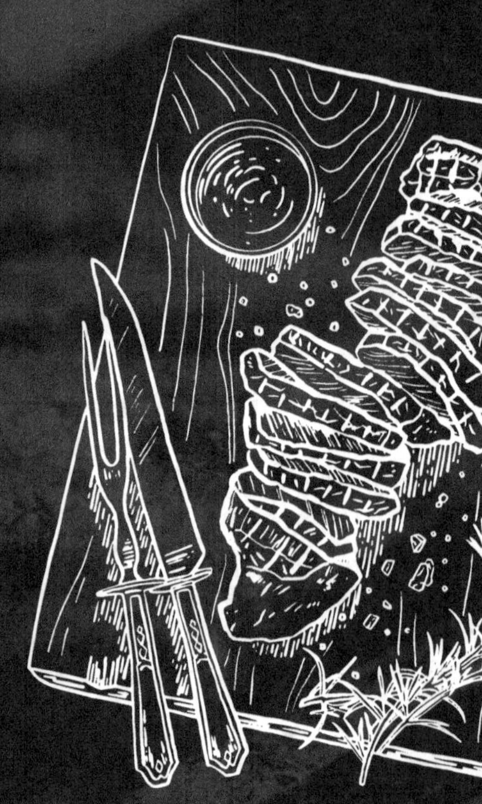

INTRODUCTION

DISCOVER THE BARBECUE MASTER WITHIN YOU WITH THIS BOOK!GET READY TO TRANSFORM YOUR BACKYARD INTO A TASTE PARADISE; THIS IS YOUR ULTIMATE PASSPORT TO BECOMING THE KING OR QUEEN OF THE GRILL! ARE YOU READY TO DAZZLE EVERYONE WITH DISHES THAT DEFY EXPECTATIONS AND TURN EVERY GATHERING INTO AN UNFORGETTABLE OCCASION?

WITH CAREFULLY SELECTED RECIPES FOR MEAT, FISH, AND VEGETABLES, THIS BOOK WILL NOT ONLY TEACH YOU HOW TO COOK CLASSIC CUTS LIKE A TRUE BARBECUE CHEF BUT WILL ALSO OPEN THE DOORS TO A WORLD OF INNOVATIVE AND CAPTIVATING FLAVORS THAT WILL SURPRISE YOUR PALATE.

FROM AROMATIC RUBS TO IRRESISTIBLE MARINADES, YOU'LL DISCOVER THE SECRETS TO FLAVORING EVERY TYPE OF MEAT, ENSURING JUICY AND FLAVORFUL RESULTS. BUT IT DOESN'T STOP THERE! OUR SECTIONS DEDICATED TO FISH, GRILLED VEGETABLES, AND SIDES ARE PERFECT FOR ROUNDING OUT YOUR MENU WITH A TOUCH OF SOPHISTICATION AND AUTHENTIC TASTE. AND WHY NOT FINISH IN STYLE?

SURPRISE YOUR GUESTS WITH OUR GRILLED DESSERTS, CREATIVE AND DELICIOUS IDEAS THAT WILL TURN YOUR BARBECUE INTO A FEAST FOR ALL THE SENSES.

BBQ COOKBOOK IS MORE THAN JUST A RECIPE BOOK: IT'S AN INVITATION TO EXPLORE, TO EXPERIMENT, AND TO CELEBRATE THE ART OF BARBECUE WITH FRIENDS AND FAMILY. GRAB YOUR TONGS, FIRE UP THE GRILL, AND GET READY TO MAKE YOUR MARK – ONE RECIPE AT A TIME!

RUBS AND MARINADES

ALL-PURPOSE BBQ RUB

INGREDIENTS

- ¼ CUP OF BROWN SUGAR
- ¼ CUP OF PAPRIKA
- 3 TABLESPOONS OF COARSE SALT
- 2 TABLESPOONS OF GROUND BLACK PEPPER
- 1 TABLESPOON OF GARLIC POWDER
- 1 TABLESPOON OF ONION POWDER
- 1 TABLESPOON OF DRIED MUSTARD
- 1 TEASPOON OF CAYENNE PEPPER (ADJUST ACCORDING TO HEAT PREFERENCE)
- 1 TEASPOON OF GROUND CUMIN
- 1 TEASPOON OF SMOKED PAPRIKA (OPTIONAL, FOR EXTRA SMOKINESS)

INSTRUCTIONS

- **MIX DRY INGREDIENTS:** IN A MIXING BOWL, COMBINE THE BROWN SUGAR, PAPRIKA, COARSE SALT, GROUND BLACK PEPPER, GARLIC POWDER, ONION POWDER, DRIED MUSTARD, CAYENNE PEPPER, GROUND CUMIN, AND SMOKED PAPRIKA IF USING. MIX THOROUGHLY TO ENSURE THAT ALL INGREDIENTS ARE EVENLY DISTRIBUTED. BREAK UP ANY CLUMPS OF BROWN SUGAR TO ENSURE A SMOOTH, EVEN RUB.

- **STORAGE:** TRANSFER THE RUB TO AN AIRTIGHT CONTAINER. THIS WILL HELP KEEP THE RUB FRESH AND PREVENT IT FROM CLUMPING DUE TO MOISTURE. THE RUB CAN BE STORED IN A COOL, DRY PLACE AND WILL REMAIN FRESH FOR UP TO 6 MONTHS.

- **APPLICATION:** WHEN YOU'RE READY TO USE THE RUB, GENEROUSLY COAT YOUR MEAT OF CHOICE ON ALL SIDES. THE SUGARS AND SPICES WILL CREATE A FLAVORFUL CRUST AS THE MEAT COOKS. FOR THE BEST RESULTS, APPLY THE RUB AT LEAST 30 MINUTES BEFORE COOKING TO ALLOW THE FLAVORS TO PENETRATE THE MEAT. FOR AN EVEN DEEPER FLAVOR, YOU CAN RUB THE MEAT AND THEN REFRIGERATE IT OVERNIGHT BEFORE COOKING.

- **COOKING:** COOK YOUR MEAT AS PLANNED, WHETHER YOU'RE GRILLING, SMOKING, OR ROASTING. THIS ALL-PURPOSE RUB IS ESPECIALLY GOOD FOR CREATING A FLAVORFUL CRUST ON THE OUTSIDE WHILE KEEPING THE INSIDE JUICY AND TENDER.

SWEET AND SPICY CHICKEN RUB

INGREDIENTS

- ¼ CUP BROWN SUGAR
- 2 TABLESPOONS PAPRIKA (USE A MIX OF SWEET AND SMOKED PAPRIKA FOR DEPTH)
- 1 TABLESPOON CHILI POWDER
- 1 TABLESPOON GARLIC POWDER
- 1 TABLESPOON ONION POWDER
- 2 TEASPOONS SALT
- 2 TEASPOONS BLACK PEPPER
- 1 TEASPOON CAYENNE PEPPER (ADJUST ACCORDING TO HEAT PREFERENCE)
- 1 TEASPOON DRIED OREGANO
- ½ TEASPOON GROUND CINNAMON

INSTRUCTIONS

- **COMBINE INGREDIENTS:** IN A MEDIUM BOWL, MIX TOGETHER THE BROWN SUGAR, PAPRIKA, CHILI POWDER, GARLIC POWDER, ONION POWDER, SALT, BLACK PEPPER, CAYENNE PEPPER, DRIED OREGANO, AND GROUND CINNAMON UNTIL WELL COMBINED. ENSURE THERE ARE NO CLUMPS, ESPECIALLY FROM THE BROWN SUGAR, TO ACHIEVE A SMOOTH AND EVEN RUB.

- **STORAGE:** TRANSFER THE RUB TO AN AIRTIGHT CONTAINER. THIS RUB CAN BE STORED IN A COOL, DRY PLACE AWAY FROM DIRECT SUNLIGHT. IT WILL KEEP FRESH FOR UP TO 6 MONTHS, READY FOR YOUR NEXT BBQ OR COOKING SESSION.

- **APPLICATION:** LIBERALLY APPLY THE RUB TO THE SURFACE OF YOUR CHICKEN OR TURKEY. FOR BEST RESULTS, GENTLY MASSAGE THE RUB UNDERNEATH THE SKIN AS WELL AS ON THE OUTSIDE. THIS ENSURES THE FLAVORS PENETRATE DEEP INTO THE MEAT. ALLOW THE POULTRY TO REST WITH THE RUB FOR AT LEAST 30 MINUTES BEFORE COOKING. FOR AN EVEN RICHER FLAVOR, LET IT MARINATE IN THE REFRIGERATOR OVERNIGHT.

- **COOKING:** PREPARE YOUR GRILL, SMOKER, OR OVEN. COOK THE POULTRY AS DESIRED, MAKING SURE TO ACHIEVE A GOOD BALANCE OF INTERNAL JUICINESS AND EXTERNAL CRISPINESS. THE SUGAR IN THE RUB WILL CARAMELIZE UNDER HEAT, FORMING A DELIGHTFUL CRUST THAT'S BOTH SWEET AND SPICY.

RICH COFFEE RUB FOR BEEF

INGREDIENTS

- ¼ CUP FINELY GROUND COFFEE
- 2 TABLESPOONS DARK BROWN SUGAR
- 2 TABLESPOONS SMOKED PAPRIKA
- 1 TABLESPOON COARSE SALT
- 1 TABLESPOON BLACK PEPPER, FRESHLY GROUND
- 1 TABLESPOON GARLIC POWDER
- 1 TABLESPOON ONION POWDER
- 1 TEASPOON CAYENNE PEPPER (ADJUST ACCORDING TO TASTE)
- 1 TEASPOON GROUND CUMIN
- ½ TEASPOON DRIED OREGANO

INSTRUCTIONS

- <u>MIX INGREDIENTS:</u> IN A BOWL, COMBINE THE FINELY GROUND COFFEE, DARK BROWN SUGAR, SMOKED PAPRIKA, COARSE SALT, FRESHLY GROUND BLACK PEPPER, GARLIC POWDER, ONION POWDER, CAYENNE PEPPER, GROUND CUMIN, AND DRIED OREGANO. MIX THOROUGHLY TO ENSURE ALL COMPONENTS ARE EVENLY DISTRIBUTED, BREAKING UP ANY CLUMPS THAT MAY FORM.

- <u>STORE FOR FRESHNESS:</u> TRANSFER THE MIXED RUB TO AN AIRTIGHT CONTAINER. STORED IN A COOL, DRY PLACE, THE RUB CAN LAST UP TO 6 MONTHS, MAINTAINING ITS POTENT FLAVORS READY FOR YOUR NEXT BARBECUE ADVENTURE.

- <u>APPLICATION:</u> GENEROUSLY APPLY THE COFFEE RUB TO YOUR BEEF CUTS, PRESSING THE MIXTURE INTO THE MEAT TO ADHERE WELL. FOR STEAKS, ALLOW THE RUB TO SIT ON THE MEAT FOR AT LEAST 30 MINUTES TO 1 HOUR BEFORE COOKING. FOR BRISKET, CONSIDER APPLYING THE RUB AND THEN REFRIGERATING OVERNIGHT TO LET THE FLAVORS PENETRATE DEEPLY.

- <u>COOKING:</u> WHETHER YOU'RE GRILLING STEAKS OR SLOW-SMOKING A BRISKET, COOK YOUR MEAT TO THE DESIRED DONENESS. THE RUB WILL CREATE A RICH, DARK CRUST THAT IS NOT ONLY VISUALLY APPEALING BUT ALSO PACKED WITH FLAVOR. REMEMBER, THE SUGARS IN THE RUB CAN BURN, SO MANAGE YOUR HEAT ACCORDINGLY, ESPECIALLY WHEN GRILLING.

LEMON-HERB RUB FOR LAMB

INGREDIENTS

- ZEST OF 2 LARGE LEMONS
- ¼ CUP FRESH ROSEMARY, FINELY CHOPPED
- ¼ CUP FRESH THYME, LEAVES ONLY
- 2 TABLESPOONS FRESH OREGANO, CHOPPED
- 2 TABLESPOONS COARSE SEA SALT
- 1 TABLESPOON GARLIC POWDER
- 1 TABLESPOON ONION POWDER
- 2 TEASPOONS FRESHLY GROUND BLACK PEPPER
- 1 TEASPOON CRUSHED RED PEPPER FLAKES (OPTIONAL, FOR A HINT OF HEAT)

INSTRUCTIONS

- **PREPARE THE INGREDIENTS:** START BY ZESTING THE LEMONS, ENSURING TO ONLY GET THE YELLOW PART OF THE PEEL WITHOUT THE BITTER WHITE PITH. FINELY CHOP THE ROSEMARY, THYME, AND OREGANO TO RELEASE THEIR AROMATIC OILS.

- **COMBINE THE RUB:** IN A MEDIUM BOWL, MIX TOGETHER THE LEMON ZEST, CHOPPED ROSEMARY, THYME LEAVES, OREGANO, COARSE SEA SALT, GARLIC POWDER, ONION POWDER, FRESHLY GROUND BLACK PEPPER, AND CRUSHED RED PEPPER FLAKES IF USING. STIR UNTIL ALL THE INGREDIENTS ARE WELL COMBINED AND THE MIXTURE IS FRAGRANT.

- **STORE APPROPRIATELY:** IF NOT USING IMMEDIATELY, STORE THE RUB IN AN AIRTIGHT CONTAINER IN THE REFRIGERATOR. THE FRESHNESS OF THE HERBS MAKES THIS RUB BEST USED WITHIN A FEW DAYS, THOUGH THE LEMON ZEST MAY DRY OUT AND FURTHER INTENSIFY THE FLAVORS OVER TIME.

- **APPLICATION:** GENEROUSLY APPLY THE LEMON-HERB RUB TO YOUR LAMB CUTS, RUBBING THE MIXTURE IN THOROUGHLY ON ALL SIDES. FOR BEST RESULTS, LET THE LAMB MARINATE WITH THE RUB FOR AT LEAST AN HOUR, OR OVERNIGHT IN THE REFRIGERATOR, TO ALLOW THE FLAVORS TO FULLY PERMEATE THE MEAT.

- **COOKING:** COOK THE LAMB AS DESIRED, WHETHER GRILLING, ROASTING, OR BROILING. THE RUB WILL CREATE A BEAUTIFULLY AROMATIC AND FLAVORFUL CRUST THAT COMPLEMENTS THE NATURAL TASTE OF THE LAMB. BE MINDFUL OF COOKING TEMPERATURES TO AVOID BURNING THE HERBS AND LEMON ZEST.

CITRUS AND HERB MARINADE

INGREDIENTS

- JUICE OF 2 LEMONS
- JUICE OF 2 LIMES
- ¼ CUP OLIVE OIL
- ¼ CUP FRESH PARSLEY, FINELY CHOPPED
- 2 TABLESPOONS FRESH ROSEMARY, FINELY CHOPPED
- 2 TABLESPOONS FRESH THYME, LEAVES ONLY
- 4 GARLIC CLOVES, MINCED
- 1 TABLESPOON HONEY OR AGAVE SYRUP (OPTIONAL, FOR A HINT OF SWEETNESS)
- 1 TEASPOON COARSE SALT
- ½ TEASPOON FRESHLY GROUND BLACK PEPPER

INSTRUCTIONS

- **MIX THE MARINADE:** IN A LARGE BOWL, WHISK TOGETHER THE LEMON JUICE, LIME JUICE, OLIVE OIL, CHOPPED PARSLEY, ROSEMARY, THYME LEAVES, MINCED GARLIC, HONEY (IF USING), COARSE SALT, AND BLACK PEPPER UNTIL WELL COMBINED. THE HONEY ADDS A SUBTLE SWEETNESS THAT BALANCES THE ACIDITY OF THE CITRUS JUICES.

- **PREPARE THE POULTRY:** PLACE YOUR CHICKEN OR TURKEY PIECES IN A LARGE RESEALABLE PLASTIC BAG OR A SHALLOW DISH. IF USING A WHOLE BIRD, CONSIDER LOOSENING THE SKIN AND APPLYING SOME OF THE MARINADE DIRECTLY UNDERNEATH FOR DEEPER FLAVOR INFUSION.

- **MARINATE:** POUR THE MARINADE OVER THE POULTRY, MAKING SURE ALL PIECES ARE WELL COATED. SEAL THE BAG OR COVER THE DISH, THEN REFRIGERATE. MARINATE FOR AT LEAST 2 HOURS, OR FOR BEST RESULTS, OVERNIGHT. THE LONGER MARINATION TIME ALLOWS THE ACIDS TO GENTLY BREAK DOWN THE PROTEINS, RESULTING IN TENDER MEAT AND MORE PRONOUNCED FLAVORS.

- **COOKING:** REMOVE THE POULTRY FROM THE MARINADE AND LET ANY EXCESS DRIP OFF. DISCARD THE REMAINING MARINADE. COOK THE POULTRY ACCORDING TO YOUR PREFERRED METHOD. THE HIGH HEAT WILL CARAMELIZE THE NATURAL SUGARS IN THE CITRUS AND HONEY, CREATING A BEAUTIFUL GOLDEN EXTERIOR.

SOY AND GINGER MARINADE

INGREDIENTS

- ½ CUP SOY SAUCE (LOW SODIUM PREFERRED)
- ¼ CUP BROWN SUGAR
- ¼ CUP OLIVE OIL
- 3 TABLESPOONS FRESHLY GRATED GINGER
- 2 TABLESPOONS RICE VINEGAR
- 2 TABLESPOONS SESAME OIL
- 4 GARLIC CLOVES, MINCED
- 1 TEASPOON GROUND BLACK PEPPER
- 1 TEASPOON ONION POWDER
- 1 GREEN ONION, FINELY CHOPPED (FOR GARNISH AND ADDED FLAVOR)
- 1 TABLESPOON TOASTED SESAME SEEDS (OPTIONAL, FOR GARNISH)

INSTRUCTIONS

- **COMBINE MARINADE INGREDIENTS:** IN A MIXING BOWL, WHISK TOGETHER THE SOY SAUCE, BROWN SUGAR, OLIVE OIL, GRATED GINGER, RICE VINEGAR, SESAME OIL, MINCED GARLIC, GROUND BLACK PEPPER, AND ONION POWDER UNTIL THE SUGAR HAS DISSOLVED AND ALL INGREDIENTS ARE WELL BLENDED.

- **PREPARE THE BEEF:** PLACE YOUR BEEF CUTS IN A LARGE RESEALABLE PLASTIC BAG OR A SHALLOW DISH. FOR MORE UNIFORM FLAVOR PENETRATION, PIERCE THE MEAT LIGHTLY WITH A FORK ALL OVER.

- **MARINATE THE BEEF:** POUR THE MARINADE OVER THE BEEF, ENSURING EVERY PIECE IS THOROUGHLY COATED. IF USING A BAG, SQUEEZE OUT AS MUCH AIR AS POSSIBLE AND SEAL IT; IF USING A DISH, COVER IT WITH PLASTIC WRAP. REFRIGERATE AND LET MARINATE FOR AT LEAST 4 HOURS, THOUGH OVERNIGHT IS RECOMMENDED FOR DEEPER FLAVOR INFUSION AND OPTIMAL TENDERNESS.

- **COOKING:** REMOVE THE BEEF FROM THE MARINADE, ALLOWING EXCESS TO DRIP OFF. DISCARD THE REMAINING MARINADE. COOK THE BEEF ACCORDING TO YOUR PREFERRED METHOD. THE SUGARS IN THE MARINADE WILL HELP CREATE A BEAUTIFUL SEAR AND CARAMELIZATION WHEN COOKED AT HIGH HEAT.

SPICY YOGURT MARINADE

INGREDIENTS

- 1 CUP PLAIN GREEK YOGURT
- 2 TABLESPOONS OLIVE OIL
- 2 TABLESPOONS LEMON JUICE
- 2 TABLESPOONS PAPRIKA (SWEET OR SMOKED, DEPENDING ON PREFERENCE)
- 1 TABLESPOON CUMIN
- 1 TABLESPOON CORIANDER
- 2 TEASPOONS TURMERIC
- 1 TEASPOON CAYENNE PEPPER (ADJUST ACCORDING TO SPICE PREFERENCE)
- 1 TEASPOON GARLIC POWDER
- 1 TEASPOON ONION POWDER
- SALT AND BLACK PEPPER TO TASTE
- 2 TABLESPOONS FRESH MINT, FINELY CHOPPED (OPTIONAL FOR ADDITIONAL FRESHNESS)

INSTRUCTIONS

- **PREPARE THE MARINADE:** IN A LARGE BOWL, COMBINE THE GREEK YOGURT, OLIVE OIL, LEMON JUICE, PAPRIKA, CUMIN, CORIANDER, TURMERIC, CAYENNE PEPPER, GARLIC POWDER, ONION POWDER, AND A GENEROUS PINCH OF SALT AND BLACK PEPPER. WHISK UNTIL ALL THE INGREDIENTS ARE WELL BLENDED AND THE MIXTURE IS SMOOTH. STIR IN THE CHOPPED MINT IF USING, FOR AN EXTRA LAYER OF FRESHNESS.

- **MARINATE THE LAMB:** PLACE THE LAMB CUTS OR CHUNKS IN A LARGE RESEALABLE PLASTIC BAG OR A NON-REACTIVE (GLASS OR CERAMIC) DISH. POUR THE MARINADE OVER THE LAMB, ENSURING THAT EVERY PIECE IS COATED THOROUGHLY. IF USING A BAG, SEAL IT TIGHTLY AFTER PRESSING OUT THE EXCESS AIR. IF USING A DISH, COVER IT WITH CLING FILM.

- **REFRIGERATE:** ALLOW THE LAMB TO MARINATE IN THE REFRIGERATOR FOR AT LEAST 4 HOURS, THOUGH OVERNIGHT MARINATION IS HIGHLY RECOMMENDED FOR THE BEST FLAVOR AND TENDERNESS. THE LONGER IT MARINATES, THE MORE PRONOUNCED THE FLAVORS WILL BE.

- **COOKING:** REMOVE THE LAMB FROM THE MARINADE, WIPING OFF ANY EXCESS. DO NOT RINSE. COOK ACCORDING TO YOUR PREFERRED METHOD, WHETHER GRILLING, ROASTING, OR BROILING. THE YOGURT IN THE MARINADE WILL HELP KEEP THE LAMB MOIST AND TENDER WHILE FORMING A DELICIOUSLY SPICED CRUST AS IT COOKS.

APPLE CIDER VINEGAR AND MUSTARD MARINADE

INGREDIENTS

- ½ CUP APPLE CIDER VINEGAR
- ¼ CUP DIJON MUSTARD
- ¼ CUP OLIVE OIL
- 2 TABLESPOONS HONEY OR BROWN SUGAR (ADJUST BASED ON DESIRED SWEETNESS)
- 4 GARLIC CLOVES, MINCED
- 1 TABLESPOON SOY SAUCE
- 1 TEASPOON SMOKED PAPRIKA
- 1 TEASPOON BLACK PEPPER
- ½ TEASPOON SALT
- 1 TEASPOON DRIED THYME OR ROSEMARY (OPTIONAL, FOR AN HERBAL NOTE)
- 2 TABLESPOONS FRESH PARSLEY, FINELY CHOPPED (FOR GARNISH AND ADDED FLAVOR)

INSTRUCTIONS

- **WHISK TOGETHER MARINADE INGREDIENTS:** IN A BOWL, COMBINE THE APPLE CIDER VINEGAR, DIJON MUSTARD, OLIVE OIL, HONEY (OR BROWN SUGAR), MINCED GARLIC, SOY SAUCE, SMOKED PAPRIKA, BLACK PEPPER, SALT, AND YOUR CHOICE OF DRIED THYME OR ROSEMARY IF USING. WHISK UNTIL THE INGREDIENTS ARE THOROUGHLY MIXED AND THE HONEY OR SUGAR HAS DISSOLVED COMPLETELY.

- **PREPARE THE PORK:** PLACE YOUR PORK CUTS IN A LARGE RESEALABLE PLASTIC BAG OR A SHALLOW NON-REACTIVE DISH. POUR THE MARINADE OVER THE PORK, MAKING SURE ALL PIECES ARE WELL COATED. IF USING A BAG, SEAL IT WHILE PRESSING OUT AS MUCH AIR AS POSSIBLE; IF USING A DISH, COVER IT WITH PLASTIC WRAP.

- **MARINATE:** REFRIGERATE THE PORK IN THE MARINADE FOR AT LEAST 4 HOURS, THOUGH OVERNIGHT MARINATION IS RECOMMENDED FOR DEEPER FLAVOR PENETRATION AND OPTIMAL TENDERNESS. THE ACID IN THE VINEGAR WILL TENDERIZE THE MEAT, WHILE THE FLAVORS MELD TOGETHER.

- **COOKING:** REMOVE THE PORK FROM THE MARINADE, LETTING EXCESS DRIP OFF (DO NOT RINSE). DISCARD THE USED MARINADE. COOK THE PORK AS PREFERRED GRILLING, ROASTING, OR PAN-SEARING. THE MARINADE WILL CARAMELIZE BEAUTIFULLY, CREATING A DELICIOUSLY TANGY AND SAVORY CRUST.

MEAT RECIPES

THE ULTIMATE GRILLED BURGER

SERVED: 4-6   COOK TIME: 6-8 MIN   TOTAL TIME: 30 MIN

INGREDIENTS

FOR THE BURGER PATTIES:

- 2 POUNDS GROUND BEEF (80/20 MIX FOR BEST FLAVOR)
- 1 TABLESPOON WORCESTERSHIRE SAUCE
- 1 TEASPOON GARLIC POWDER
- SALT AND FRESHLY GROUND BLACK PEPPER
- 1 TEASPOON ONION POWDER

FOR SERVING:

- 4-6 HAMBURGER BUNS, TOASTED
- LETTUCE LEAVES
- TOMATO SLICES
- RED ONION SLICES
- PICKLES
- CHEDDAR CHEESE SLICES (OR YOUR CHOICE OF CHEESE)
- KETCHUP, MUSTARD, AND MAYONNAISE

OPTIONAL GOURMET TOPPINGS:

- CRISPY BACON, SAUTÉED MUSHROOMS, AVOCADO SLICES, OR BLUE CHEESE

INSTRUCTIONS

- **PREPARE THE PATTIES:** IN A LARGE BOWL, COMBINE THE GROUND BEEF, WORCESTERSHIRE SAUCE, GARLIC POWDER, ONION POWDER, SALT, AND BLACK PEPPER. MIX GENTLY TO COMBINE. OVER-MIXING WILL TOUGHEN THE PATTIES. DIVIDE THE MIXTURE INTO 4-6 EQUAL PORTIONS, DEPENDING ON DESIRED PATTY SIZE. SHAPE EACH PORTION INTO A ROUND, FLAT PATTY THAT'S ABOUT 1 INCH THICK. PRESS A SMALL INDENT IN THE CENTER OF EACH PATTY WITH YOUR THUMB – THIS PREVENTS THE PATTIES FROM PUFFING UP IN THE CENTER AS THEY COOK.

- **PREHEAT THE GRILL:** PREHEAT YOUR GRILL TO HIGH HEAT. ENSURE GRATES ARE CLEAN AND LIGHTLY OILED TO PREVENT STICKING.

- **GRILL THE BURGERS:** PLACE THE PATTIES ON THE GRILL AND COOK FOR ABOUT 3-4 MINUTES ON ONE SIDE. FLIP THE PATTIES, ADD CHEESE IF USING, AND COOK FOR ANOTHER 3-4 MINUTES FOR MEDIUM-RARE TO MEDIUM, OR LONGER FOR WELL-DONE. AVOID PRESSING DOWN ON THE BURGERS WHILE COOKING AS THIS SQUEEZES OUT THE JUICES.

- **TOAST THE BUNS:** DURING THE LAST FEW MINUTES OF COOKING, PLACE THE BUNS CUT-SIDE DOWN ON THE GRILL TO TOAST LIGHTLY.

- **ASSEMBLE THE BURGERS:** ON THE BOTTOM HALF OF EACH TOASTED BUN, SPREAD A LAYER OF MAYONNAISE, ADD A LEAF OF LETTUCE, A SLICE OF TOMATO, AND A SLICE OF RED ONION. PLACE THE GRILLED PATTY WITH CHEESE ON TOP OF THE ONION, THEN ADD PICKLES, AND ANY OTHER TOPPINGS YOU DESIRE. SPREAD KETCHUP AND MUSTARD ON THE TOP HALF OF THE BUN, THEN PLACE IT ON TOP OF THE BURGER.

- **SERVE:** SERVE THE BURGERS IMMEDIATELY, WITH SIDES LIKE POTATO CHIPS, FRIES, OR A SIMPLE SALAD.

GARLIC BUTTER RIBEYE STEAK

SERVED: 2   COOK TIME: 10 MIN   TOTAL TIME: 50 MIN

INGREDIENTS

- 2 RIBEYE STEAKS, APPROXIMATELY 1 INCH THICK
- SALT AND FRESHLY GROUND BLACK PEPPER TO TASTE
- 2 TABLESPOONS OLIVE OIL
- 4 TABLESPOONS UNSALTED BUTTER
- 3 GARLIC CLOVES, MINCED
- 1 TEASPOON FRESH THYME LEAVES
- 1 TEASPOON FRESH ROSEMARY, FINELY CHOPPED
- OPTIONAL: 1 TABLESPOON PARSLEY, FINELY CHOPPED, FOR GARNISH

INSTRUCTIONS

- **PREPARE THE STEAKS:** LET THE STEAKS REACH ROOM TEMPERATURE, ABOUT 30 MINUTES BEFORE GRILLING. SEASON BOTH SIDES GENEROUSLY WITH SALT AND PEPPER.

- **PREHEAT THE GRILL:** HEAT YOUR GRILL TO MEDIUM-HIGH HEAT. ENSURE THE GRILL IS CLEAN AND LIGHTLY OILED TO PREVENT STICKING.

- **GRILL THE STEAKS:** BRUSH THE STEAKS WITH OLIVE OIL AND PLACE THEM ON THE GRILL. GRILL FOR ABOUT 4-5 MINUTES ON EACH SIDE FOR MEDIUM-RARE OR ADJUST THE TIME TO ACHIEVE YOUR PREFERRED DONENESS. LOOK FOR GOOD GRILL MARKS BEFORE FLIPPING.

- **MAKE THE GARLIC BUTTER SAUCE:** IN A SMALL SAUCEPAN ON THE GRILL SIDE BURNER (OR MADE IN ADVANCE ON THE STOVE), MELT THE BUTTER AND ADD THE MINCED GARLIC, THYME, AND ROSEMARY. COOK UNTIL THE GARLIC IS FRAGRANT. SPOON THE MELTED GARLIC BUTTER OVER THE STEAKS DURING THE LAST MINUTE OF GRILLING TO BASTE THEM.

- **REST THE STEAKS:** TRANSFER THE STEAKS TO A PLATE AND LET THEM REST FOR ABOUT 5 MINUTES. THIS HELPS THE JUICES REDISTRIBUTE THROUGHOUT THE MEAT FOR A JUICIER STEAK.

- **SERVE:** PLACE THE STEAKS ON PLATES AND DRIZZLE WITH THE REMAINING GARLIC BUTTER SAUCE. GARNISH WITH CHOPPED PARSLEY IF USING.

HERB-CRUSTED BEEF ROAST

SERVED: 6-8   TOTAL TIME: 2-3,5 HOURS

INGREDIENTS

- 3 TO 4-POUND BEEF ROAST (SUCH AS SIRLOIN TIP, RUMP, OR TENDERLOIN)
- 2 TABLESPOONS OLIVE OIL
- 2 TABLESPOONS FRESH ROSEMARY, FINELY CHOPPED
- 2 TABLESPOONS FRESH THYME, FINELY CHOPPED
- 2 TABLESPOONS FRESH OREGANO, FINELY CHOPPED
- 4 GARLIC CLOVES, MINCED
- 1 TABLESPOON COARSE SEA SALT
- 1 TABLESPOON FRESHLY GROUND BLACK PEPPER
- 1 TEASPOON SMOKED PAPRIKA (OPTIONAL FOR A SMOKY FLAVOR)

INSTRUCTIONS

- **PREPARE THE HERB CRUST:** IN A SMALL BOWL, COMBINE THE CHOPPED ROSEMARY, THYME, OREGANO, MINCED GARLIC, COARSE SEA SALT, FRESHLY GROUND BLACK PEPPER, AND SMOKED PAPRIKA IF USING. MIX IN THE OLIVE OIL TO CREATE A THICK PASTE.

- **SEASON THE ROAST:** RUB THE HERB MIXTURE ALL OVER THE BEEF ROAST, ENSURING IT'S EVENLY COATED ON ALL SIDES. ALLOW THE ROAST TO SIT AT ROOM TEMPERATURE FOR ABOUT 30 MINUTES BEFORE GRILLING. THIS HELPS THE BEEF COOK MORE EVENLY.

- **PREHEAT THE GRILL:** PREHEAT YOUR GRILL FOR INDIRECT GRILLING OVER LOW HEAT. YOU'RE AIMING FOR A GRILL TEMPERATURE AROUND 275°F TO 300°F (135°C TO 150°C). ON A CHARCOAL GRILL, ARRANGE THE COALS ON ONE SIDE OF THE GRILL AND COOK THE MEAT ON THE OTHER SIDE. ON A GAS GRILL, LIGHT THE BURNERS ON ONE SIDE TO MEDIUM-LOW AND PLACE THE MEAT ON THE OTHER SIDE.

- **SLOW-GRILL THE ROAST:** PLACE THE BEEF ROAST ON THE GRILL OVER INDIRECT HEAT. CLOSE THE LID AND COOK SLOWLY, TURNING OCCASIONALLY, UNTIL THE INTERNAL TEMPERATURE REACHES YOUR DESIRED LEVEL OF DONENESS (ABOUT 125°F TO 130°F FOR MEDIUM-RARE, DEPENDING ON THE CUT AND YOUR PREFERENCE). THIS COULD TAKE 2 TO 3 HOURS, DEPENDING ON THE SIZE OF THE ROAST AND GRILL TEMPERATURE.

- **REST BEFORE SLICING:** REMOVE THE ROAST FROM THE GRILL AND LET IT REST FOR AT LEAST 20 MINUTES BEFORE SLICING. THIS ALLOWS THE JUICES TO REDISTRIBUTE THROUGHOUT THE MEAT, ENSURING IT'S MOIST AND FLAVORFUL.

- **SERVE:** SLICE THE ROAST AGAINST THE GRAIN INTO THIN OR THICK SLICES, AS PREFERRED. THE HERB CRUST SHOULD BE FRAGRANT AND FLAVORFUL, PROVIDING A PERFECT COMPLEMENT TO THE TENDER, JUICY BEEF.

TEXAS-STYLE BRISKET BBQ

SERVED: 8-10   TOTAL TIME: 9-12 HOURS

INGREDIENTS

- 1 WHOLE BRISKET (10 TO 12 POUNDS) WITH FAT CAP TRIMMED TO ABOUT ¼ INCH
- ¼ CUP COARSE SALT
- ¼ CUP BLACK PEPPER, FRESHLY GROUND
- 2 TABLESPOONS PAPRIKA
- 1 TABLESPOON ONION POWDER
- 1 TABLESPOON GARLIC POWDER
- 1 TEASPOON CAYENNE PEPPER (OPTIONAL, FOR A KICK)

INSTRUCTIONS

- **PREPARE THE BRISKET:** THE NIGHT BEFORE YOU PLAN TO GRILL, PREPARE THE BRISKET BY TRIMMING THE FAT CAP TO ABOUT ¼ INCH THICKNESS. THIS HELPS TO KEEP THE BRISKET MOIST WHILE ALLOWING THE SMOKE AND RUB TO PENETRATE THE MEAT.

- **APPLY THE RUB:** MIX ALL THE RUB INGREDIENTS IN A BOWL. COAT THE BRISKET EVENLY WITH THE RUB, MAKING SURE BOTH SIDES AND ALL EDGES ARE COVERED. WRAP THE BRISKET IN BUTCHER PAPER OR PLASTIC WRAP AND REFRIGERATE OVERNIGHT TO ALLOW THE FLAVORS TO MELD.

- **PREHEAT THE GRILL:** ON THE DAY OF COOKING, PREHEAT YOUR GRILL TO A CONSISTENT 225°F TO 250°F. IF USING WOOD CHIPS, SOAK THEM IN WATER BEFOREHAND AND PLACE THEM IN THE SMOKER BOX OR DIRECTLY ON THE COALS.

- **GRILL THE BRISKET:** PLACE THE BRISKET FAT SIDE UP ON THE GRILL AWAY FROM DIRECT HEAT (INDIRECT COOKING METHOD). MAINTAIN A CONSISTENT TEMPERATURE BY MONITORING AND ADJUSTING THE GRILL AS NEEDED. ADD WOOD CHIPS AS NECESSARY TO MAINTAIN SMOKE.

- **MONITOR THE TEMPERATURE:** KEEP THE GRILL COVERED AND SMOKE THE BRISKET UNTIL IT REACHES AN INTERNAL TEMPERATURE OF AROUND 200°F TO 205°F, WHICH COULD TAKE ABOUT 6 TO 8 HOURS DEPENDING ON THE SIZE OF THE BRISKET AND CONSISTENCY OF THE GRILL TEMPERATURE.

- **REST THE BRISKET:** ONCE THE BRISKET REACHES THE DESIRED INTERNAL TEMPERATURE, REMOVE IT FROM THE GRILL AND LET IT REST FOR AT LEAST 1 HOUR BEFORE SLICING. WRAPPING IT IN BUTCHER PAPER OR FOIL DURING THIS TIME CAN HELP RETAIN MOISTURE.

- **SLICE AND SERVE:** SLICE THE BRISKET AGAINST THE GRAIN INTO THIN SLICES. THE BRISKET SHOULD BE TENDER ENOUGH TO PULL APART WITH A GENTLE TUG, WITH A SMOKY CRUST (BARK) ON THE OUTSIDE AND JUICY, FLAVORFUL MEAT ON THE INSIDE.

ST. LOUIS STYLE RIBS

SERVED: 4-6   TOTAL TIME: 3-4 HOURS

INGREDIENTS

- 2 RACKS ST. LOUIS STYLE RIBS (ABOUT 2-3 POUNDS EACH)
- 1/4 CUP OF YOUR FAVORITE BBQ DRY RUB
- 1 CUP BBQ SAUCE
- OLIVE OIL, FOR BRUSHING

INSTRUCTIONS

- **PREPARE THE RIBS:** REMOVE THE MEMBRANE FROM THE BACK OF THE RIBS FOR BETTER FLAVOR ABSORPTION AND TENDERNESS. BRUSH THE RIBS LIGHTLY WITH OLIVE OIL AND THEN GENEROUSLY APPLY THE DRY RUB ALL OVER THE RIBS.

- **PREHEAT THE GRILL:** PREHEAT YOUR GRILL TO MEDIUM HEAT (AROUND 300°F). IF YOUR GRILL HAS A TEMPERATURE GAUGE, AIM TO MAINTAIN THIS TEMPERATURE THROUGHOUT THE COOKING PROCESS.

- **GRILL THE RIBS:** PLACE THE RIBS BONE-SIDE DOWN ON THE GRILL AWAY FROM DIRECT HEAT. COVER THE GRILL AND LET THE RIBS COOK FOR ABOUT 2-3 HOURS. CHECK OCCASIONALLY AND TURN THE RIBS EVERY HOUR TO ENSURE EVEN COOKING. THE RIBS ARE DONE WHEN THE MEAT IS TENDER AND PULLS AWAY FROM THE BONES.

- **APPLY THE BBQ SAUCE:** IN THE LAST 30 MINUTES OF GRILLING, START BRUSHING YOUR BBQ SAUCE OVER THE RIBS. CONTINUE TO APPLY THE SAUCE AND TURN THE RIBS EVERY 10 MINUTES TO BUILD UP A NICE LAYER OF GLAZE.

- **REST AND SERVE:** ONCE COOKED, REMOVE THE RIBS FROM THE GRILL AND LET THEM REST FOR ABOUT 10-15 MINUTES. THIS HELPS THE JUICES REDISTRIBUTE, MAKING THE MEAT MORE TENDER AND FLAVORFUL. SLICE THE RIBS BETWEEN THE BONES AND SERVE WITH ADDITIONAL BBQ SAUCE ON THE SIDE.

GRILLED BEEF CHEEKS WITH CHIMICHURRI SAUCE

SERVED: 4   COOK TIME: 3-4 HOURS   TOTAL TIME: 3-4.20 HOURS

INGREDIENTS

FOR THE BEEF CHEEKS:

- 4 BEEF CHEEKS, TRIMMED OF EXCESS FAT
- 2 TABLESPOONS OLIVE OIL
- SALT AND FRESHLY GROUND BLACK PEPPER TO TASTE
- 1 TABLESPOON SMOKED PAPRIKA

FOR THE CHIMICHURRI SAUCE:

- 1 CUP FRESH PARSLEY, FINELY CHOPPED
- 1/4 CUP FRESH CILANTRO, FINELY CHOPPED
- 3 GARLIC CLOVES, MINCED
- 1/2 CUP OLIVE OIL
- 2 TABLESPOONS RED WINE VINEGAR
- 1 TABLESPOON LIME JUICE
- 1 TEASPOON RED PEPPER FLAKES (ADJUST TO TASTE)
- SALT AND PEPPER TO TASTE

INSTRUCTIONS

- **PREPARE THE BEEF CHEEKS:** BEGIN BY TRIMMING ANY EXCESS FAT FROM THE BEEF CHEEKS. SEASON THEM GENEROUSLY WITH SALT, PEPPER, AND SMOKED PAPRIKA. DRIZZLE WITH OLIVE OIL TO COAT.

- **PREHEAT THE GRILL:** HEAT YOUR GRILL TO A MEDIUM-LOW SETTING FOR INDIRECT GRILLING. THE GOAL IS TO COOK THE BEEF CHEEKS SLOWLY TO BREAK DOWN THE CONNECTIVE TISSUES, ENSURING THEY BECOME TENDER.

- **GRILL THE BEEF CHEEKS:** PLACE THE BEEF CHEEKS ON THE COOLER PART OF THE GRILL (NOT DIRECTLY OVER THE HEAT). COVER AND COOK FOR 3-4 HOURS, TURNING OCCASIONALLY, UNTIL THEY ARE EXTREMELY TENDER. THE INTERNAL TEMPERATURE SHOULD REACH AROUND 200°F (93°C) WHEN THEY'RE DONE. IF YOU HAVE A SMOKER, YOU CAN ALSO SMOKE THEM AT 225°F (107°C) FOR A MORE PRONOUNCED SMOKY FLAVOR.

- **MAKE THE CHIMICHURRI SAUCE:** WHILE THE BEEF CHEEKS ARE GRILLING, PREPARE THE CHIMICHURRI SAUCE. IN A BOWL, COMBINE THE CHOPPED PARSLEY, CILANTRO, MINCED GARLIC, OLIVE OIL, RED WINE VINEGAR, LIME JUICE, RED PEPPER FLAKES, SALT, AND PEPPER. WHISK TOGETHER UNTIL WELL COMBINED AND SET ASIDE FOR THE FLAVORS TO MELD.

- **REST AND SLICE THE BEEF CHEEKS:** ONCE THE BEEF CHEEKS ARE TENDER, REMOVE THEM FROM THE GRILL AND LET THEM REST FOR ABOUT 10 MINUTES. THEY SHOULD BE SO TENDER THAT SLICING IS OPTIONAL; YOU CAN ALSO GENTLY PULL THEM APART WITH FORKS.

- **SERVE:** SERVE THE BEEF CHEEKS WARM, DRIZZLED WITH THE CHIMICHURRI SAUCE OR ON THE SIDE FOR DIPPING.

SPICED GRILLED CHICKEN BREAST RECIPE

SERVED: 4   **COOK TIME: 14 MIN**   **TOTAL TIME: 30 MIN**

INGREDIENTS

- 4 BONELESS, SKINLESS CHICKEN BREASTS
- 2 TABLESPOONS OLIVE OIL
- 1 TABLESPOON SMOKED PAPRIKA
- 1 TEASPOON GROUND CUMIN
- 1 TEASPOON GARLIC POWDER
- 1 TEASPOON ONION POWDER
- 1/2 TEASPOON GROUND CORIANDER
- 1/2 TEASPOON CHILI POWDER (ADJUST BASED ON HEAT PREFERENCE)
- SALT AND FRESHLY GROUND BLACK PEPPER TO TASTE
- FRESH CILANTRO OR PARSLEY, CHOPPED (FOR GARNISH)

INSTRUCTIONS

- **PREPARE THE CHICKEN:** IF THE CHICKEN BREASTS ARE VERY THICK, POUND THEM TO AN EVEN THICKNESS USING A MEAT MALLET OR ROLLING PIN. THIS HELPS THEM COOK EVENLY AND QUICKLY.

- **MIX THE SPICES:** IN A SMALL BOWL, COMBINE THE SMOKED PAPRIKA, GROUND CUMIN, GARLIC POWDER, ONION POWDER, GROUND CORIANDER, CHILI POWDER, SALT, AND BLACK PEPPER. MIX THOROUGHLY TO CREATE THE SPICE RUB.

- **SEASON THE CHICKEN:** DRIZZLE THE CHICKEN BREASTS WITH OLIVE OIL AND RUB THEM ALL OVER WITH THE SPICE MIXTURE, ENSURING THEY ARE WELL-COATED.

- **MARINATE (OPTIONAL):** FOR DEEPER FLAVOR, LET THE CHICKEN MARINATE FOR AT LEAST 30 MINUTES IN THE REFRIGERATOR, OR OVERNIGHT IF TIME ALLOWS.

- **PREHEAT THE GRILL:** HEAT YOUR GRILL TO A MEDIUM-HIGH HEAT. MAKE SURE IT'S HOT BEFORE YOU ADD THE CHICKEN TO ACHIEVE GOOD GRILL MARKS AND PREVENT STICKING.

- **GRILL THE CHICKEN:** PLACE THE CHICKEN BREASTS ON THE GRILL. COOK FOR 6-7 MINUTES ON ONE SIDE, THEN FLIP AND COOK FOR AN ADDITIONAL 5-6 MINUTES ON THE OTHER SIDE, OR UNTIL THE INTERNAL TEMPERATURE REACHES 165°F (74°C). THE COOKING TIME MAY VARY DEPENDING ON THE THICKNESS OF THE CHICKEN.

- **REST THE CHICKEN:** REMOVE THE CHICKEN FROM THE GRILL AND LET IT REST FOR A FEW MINUTES BEFORE SLICING. THIS HELPS RETAIN THE JUICES, MAKING THE CHICKEN MORE MOIST AND FLAVORFUL.

- **SERVE:** SLICE THE CHICKEN AND GARNISH WITH CHOPPED CILANTRO OR PARSLEY. SERVE HOT.

HONEY-SRIRACHA CHICKEN WINGS RECIPE

SERVED: 4-6　　**COOK TIME: 20 MIN**　　**TOTAL TIME: 35 MIN**

INGREDIENTS

FOR THE CHICKEN WINGS:

- 2 POUNDS CHICKEN WINGS, TIPS REMOVED, DRUMETTES AND FLATS SEPARATED
- 1 TABLESPOON VEGETABLE OIL
- SALT AND FRESHLY GROUND BLACK PEPPER TO TASTE

FOR THE HONEY-SRIRACHA GLAZE:

- 1/3 CUP HONEY
- 1/4 CUP SRIRACHA SAUCE
- 2 TABLESPOONS SOY SAUCE
- 1 TABLESPOON LIME JUICE
- 2 CLOVES GARLIC, MINCED
- 1 TEASPOON GINGER, GRATED (OPTIONAL FOR ADDED ZING)

INSTRUCTIONS

- **PREPARE THE WINGS:** PAT THE CHICKEN WINGS DRY WITH PAPER TOWELS TO ENSURE THEY GET CRISPY. TOSS THEM WITH VEGETABLE OIL, SALT, AND PEPPER.

- **PREHEAT THE GRILL:** HEAT YOUR GRILL TO MEDIUM-HIGH HEAT. MAKE SURE IT'S HOT TO PREVENT STICKING AND TO ACHIEVE A GOOD SEAR ON THE WINGS.

- **GRILL THE WINGS:** PLACE THE WINGS ON THE GRILL AND COOK FOR ABOUT 15-20 MINUTES, TURNING OCCASIONALLY, UNTIL THEY ARE GOLDEN BROWN AND CRISP. THE INTERNAL TEMPERATURE SHOULD REACH 165°F (74°C) WHEN THEY'RE DONE.

- **MAKE THE HONEY-SRIRACHA GLAZE:** WHILE THE WINGS ARE GRILLING, COMBINE HONEY, SRIRACHA SAUCE, SOY SAUCE, LIME JUICE, MINCED GARLIC, AND GRATED GINGER IN A SMALL SAUCEPAN. BRING THE MIXTURE TO A SIMMER OVER MEDIUM HEAT AND LET IT REDUCE SLIGHTLY UNTIL IT THICKENS INTO A GLAZE, ABOUT 5-7 MINUTES.

- **GLAZE THE WINGS:** ONCE THE WINGS ARE COOKED AND CRISPY, BRUSH THEM GENEROUSLY WITH THE HONEY-SRIRACHA GLAZE. RETURN THEM TO THE GRILL FOR AN ADDITIONAL 2-3 MINUTES TO CARAMELIZE THE GLAZE.

- **SERVE:** REMOVE THE WINGS FROM THE GRILL AND LET THEM REST FOR A FEW MINUTES. OPTIONALLY, TOSS THE WINGS WITH ANY REMAINING GLAZE FOR EXTRA FLAVOR AND SERVE WITH A SPRINKLE OF SESAME SEEDS OR CHOPPED CILANTRO FOR GARNISH.

BBQ CHICKEN THIGHS

SERVED: 8 **COOK TIME: 30 MIN** **TOTAL TIME: 45 MIN**

INGREDIENTS

FOR THE CHICKEN:

- 8 BONE-IN, SKIN-ON CHICKEN THIGHS
- SALT AND FRESHLY GROUND BLACK PEPPER TO TASTE
- 2 TABLESPOONS OLIVE OIL

FOR THE BBQ SAUCE:

- 1 CUP KETCHUP
- 1/4 CUP APPLE CIDER VINEGAR
- 1/4 CUP BROWN SUGAR
- 2 TABLESPOONS HONEY
- 1 TABLESPOON WORCESTERSHIRE SAUCE
- 1 TABLESPOON SMOKED PAPRIKA
- 1 TEASPOON GARLIC POWDER
- 1 TEASPOON ONION POWDER
- 1/2 TEASPOON CHILI POWDER (ADJUST BASED ON HEAT PREFERENCE)
- SALT AND PEPPER TO TASTE

INSTRUCTIONS

- **PREP THE CHICKEN:** PAT THE CHICKEN THIGHS DRY WITH PAPER TOWELS TO REMOVE ANY EXCESS MOISTURE. SEASON BOTH SIDES OF THE THIGHS WITH SALT AND PEPPER, THEN BRUSH THEM LIGHTLY WITH OLIVE OIL. THIS HELPS THE SKIN GET CRISPY AND GOLDEN.

- **PREPARE THE BBQ SAUCE:** IN A SAUCEPAN OVER MEDIUM HEAT, COMBINE THE KETCHUP, APPLE CIDER VINEGAR, BROWN SUGAR, HONEY, WORCESTERSHIRE SAUCE, SMOKED PAPRIKA, GARLIC POWDER, ONION POWDER, CHILI POWDER, SALT, AND PEPPER. BRING THE MIXTURE TO A SIMMER AND COOK FOR ABOUT 5-10 MINUTES UNTIL THE SAUCE THICKENS SLIGHTLY. REMOVE FROM HEAT.

- **PREHEAT THE GRILL:** HEAT YOUR GRILL TO MEDIUM-HIGH HEAT. IF USING A CHARCOAL GRILL, SET IT UP FOR INDIRECT GRILLING WITH COALS ON ONE SIDE.

- **GRILL THE CHICKEN:** PLACE THE CHICKEN THIGHS SKIN-SIDE DOWN ON THE GRILL OVER DIRECT HEAT. GRILL FOR ABOUT 5-7 MINUTES ON EACH SIDE TO GET GOOD GRILL MARKS. MOVE THE THIGHS TO INDIRECT HEAT AND CONTINUE COOKING, TURNING OCCASIONALLY, UNTIL THEY REACH AN INTERNAL TEMPERATURE OF 165°F (ABOUT 15-20 MINUTES, DEPENDING ON THEIR SIZE).

- **APPLY THE BBQ SAUCE:** DURING THE LAST 10 MINUTES OF COOKING, START BRUSHING THE CHICKEN THIGHS WITH THE BBQ SAUCE, TURNING AND BASTING THEM FREQUENTLY TO BUILD UP A NICE LAYER OF SAUCE WITHOUT BURNING IT.

- **REST AND SERVE:** REMOVE THE CHICKEN THIGHS FROM THE GRILL AND LET THEM REST FOR A FEW MINUTES BEFORE SERVING. THIS HELPS THE JUICES REDISTRIBUTE THROUGHOUT THE MEAT, KEEPING IT MOIST AND TENDER.

APPLEWOOD SMOKED TURKEY

SERVED: 12-14   COOK TIME: 7 HOURS   TOTAL TIME: 30 HOURS

INGREDIENTS

- 1 WHOLE TURKEY (12-14 POUNDS), THAWED IF PREVIOUSLY FROZEN
- 4 TABLESPOONS KOSHER SALT
- 2 TABLESPOONS BLACK PEPPER
- 2 TABLESPOONS PAPRIKA
- 1 TABLESPOON GARLIC POWDER
- 1 TABLESPOON ONION POWDER
- 2 TEASPOONS DRIED THYME
- OLIVE OIL, FOR COATING THE TURKEY
- APPLEWOOD CHIPS, SOAKED IN WATER FOR AT LEAST 30 MINUTES

BRINE (OPTIONAL BUT RECOMMENDED):

- 1 GALLON WATER
- 1 CUP KOSHER SALT
- 1/2 CUP SUGAR
- 1 ONION, QUARTERED
- 4 GARLIC CLOVES, SMASHED
- 1 TABLESPOON PEPPERCORNS

INSTRUCTIONS

- **BRINE THE TURKEY (OPTIONAL):** TO KEEP YOUR TURKEY ESPECIALLY MOIST, YOU CAN BRINE IT BEFORE SMOKING. COMBINE ALL BRINE INGREDIENTS IN A LARGE POT AND BRING TO A SIMMER, STIRRING UNTIL THE SALT AND SUGAR DISSOLVE. COOL COMPLETELY. SUBMERGE THE TURKEY IN THE BRINE, COVER, AND REFRIGERATE FOR 12 TO 24 HOURS.

- **PREPARE THE TURKEY:** REMOVE THE TURKEY FROM THE BRINE (IF USED), RINSE UNDER COLD WATER, AND PAT DRY WITH PAPER TOWELS. MIX TOGETHER THE SALT, PEPPER, PAPRIKA, GARLIC POWDER, ONION POWDER, AND DRIED THYME. RUB THE TURKEY INSIDE AND OUT WITH OLIVE OIL AND THEN APPLY THE SPICE MIXTURE GENEROUSLY.

- **PREHEAT THE SMOKER:** PREHEAT YOUR SMOKER TO 250°F (120°C). DRAIN THE APPLEWOOD CHIPS AND PLACE THEM IN THE SMOKER ACCORDING TO THE MANUFACTURER'S INSTRUCTIONS.

- **SMOKE THE TURKEY:** PLACE THE TURKEY BREAST SIDE UP ON THE SMOKER RACK. CLOSE THE LID AND SMOKE, MAINTAINING A CONSISTENT TEMPERATURE, UNTIL THE INTERNAL TEMPERATURE OF THE THICKEST PART OF THE THIGH REACHES 165°F (74°C). THIS USUALLY TAKES ABOUT 30 MINUTES PER POUND, SO A 14-POUND TURKEY MIGHT TAKE AROUND 7 HOURS.

- **REST THE TURKEY:** ONCE DONE, REMOVE THE TURKEY FROM THE SMOKER AND LET IT REST FOR AT LEAST 20 MINUTES BEFORE CARVING. THIS ALLOWS THE JUICES TO REDISTRIBUTE THROUGHOUT THE MEAT, ENSURING THE TURKEY IS MOIST AND FLAVORFUL

ULTIMATE BBQ TURKEY DELIGHT

SERVED: 4-6   **COOK TIME: 15 MIN**   **TOTAL TIME: 4 HOURS**

INGREDIENTS

- 1 WHOLE TURKEY (12-14 POUNDS), THAWED IF FROZEN
- 1/4 CUP OLIVE OIL
- 1/4 CUP MELTED BUTTER
- 1 TABLESPOON SALT
- 1 TABLESPOON BLACK PEPPER
- 1 TABLESPOON SMOKED PAPRIKA
- 1 TABLESPOON GARLIC POWDER
- 1 TABLESPOON ONION POWDER
- 2 CUPS CHICKEN BROTH (FOR BASTING AND ADDED MOISTURE)

INSTRUCTIONS

- **PREPARE THE TURKEY:** REMOVE THE GIBLETS AND NECK FROM THE TURKEY, RINSE IT INSIDE AND OUT, AND PAT DRY WITH PAPER TOWELS. LOOSEN THE SKIN OVER THE BREAST AND THIGH AREAS TO INSERT SEASONING.

- **SEASON THE TURKEY:** IN A SMALL BOWL, MIX OLIVE OIL, MELTED BUTTER, SALT, PEPPER, SMOKED PAPRIKA, GARLIC POWDER, AND ONION POWDER TO CREATE A RUB. APPLY THE RUB BOTH UNDER AND OVER THE SKIN OF THE TURKEY, AND INSIDE THE CAVITY, TO ENSURE EVEN FLAVORING.

- **PREPARE THE GRILL:** SET UP YOUR GRILL FOR INDIRECT COOKING AND PREHEAT TO A MEDIUM HEAT (ABOUT 325°F).

- **GRILL THE TURKEY:** PLACE THE TURKEY BREAST SIDE UP ON THE GRILL, AWAY FROM THE DIRECT HEAT. USE A ROASTING PAN UNDER THE TURKEY TO CATCH DRIPPINGS. CLOSE THE GRILL LID AND COOK, BASTING EVERY HOUR WITH CHICKEN BROTH TO MAINTAIN MOISTURE.

- **COOKING TIME:** THE COOKING TIME WILL BE ABOUT 2.5 TO 3 HOURS, BUT ALWAYS USE A MEAT THERMOMETER TO CHECK THE INTERNAL TEMPERATURE. THE TURKEY IS DONE WHEN THE THIGH MEAT REACHES 165°F.

- **REST AND SERVE:** LET THE TURKEY REST FOR AT LEAST 20 MINUTES BEFORE CARVING TO ALLOW THE JUICES TO REDISTRIBUTE. CARVE THE TURKEY AND SERVE WITH YOUR CHOICE OF SIDE DISHES.

SPICY TURKEY DRUMSTICKS

SERVED: 6   COOK TIME: 30 MIN   TOTAL TIME: 5 HOURS

INGREDIENTS

- 6 TURKEY DRUMSTICKS
- 2 TABLESPOONS OLIVE OIL
- 2 TABLESPOONS PAPRIKA
- 1 TABLESPOON GARLIC POWDER
- 1 TABLESPOON ONION POWDER
- 1 TABLESPOON GROUND CUMIN
- 1 TEASPOON CAYENNE PEPPER (ADJUST BASED ON YOUR HEAT PREFERENCE)
- 1 TEASPOON DRIED THYME
- SALT AND BLACK PEPPER TO TASTE
- OPTIONAL: 1 TABLESPOON BROWN SUGAR FOR A TOUCH OF SWEETNESS

FOR THE MARINADE:

- 1/4 CUP HOT SAUCE (LIKE SRIRACHA OR YOUR FAVORITE CHILI SAUCE)
- 1/4 CUP APPLE CIDER VINEGAR
- 2 TABLESPOONS SOY SAUCE
- JUICE OF 1 LIME
- 3 CLOVES GARLIC, MINCED
- 1 INCH PIECE OF GINGER, GRATED

INSTRUCTIONS

- **PREPARE THE MARINADE:** IN A LARGE BOWL, COMBINE THE HOT SAUCE, APPLE CIDER VINEGAR, SOY SAUCE, LIME JUICE, MINCED GARLIC, AND GRATED GINGER. MIX WELL TO BLEND THE FLAVORS.

- **SEASON THE DRUMSTICKS:** IN A SEPARATE BOWL, MIX TOGETHER THE OLIVE OIL, PAPRIKA, GARLIC POWDER, ONION POWDER, GROUND CUMIN, CAYENNE PEPPER, DRIED THYME, AND OPTIONALLY, BROWN SUGAR. RUB THIS SPICE MIX ALL OVER THE TURKEY DRUMSTICKS, MAKING SURE THEY ARE WELL COATED.

- **MARINATE:** PLACE THE SEASONED DRUMSTICKS INTO A LARGE RESEALABLE PLASTIC BAG OR A DEEP DISH. POUR THE MARINADE OVER THE DRUMSTICKS, ENSURING THEY ARE COMPLETELY COVERED. SEAL THE BAG OR COVER THE DISH AND REFRIGERATE FOR AT LEAST 4 HOURS, PREFERABLY OVERNIGHT, TO ALLOW THE FLAVORS TO PENETRATE DEEPLY.

- **PREHEAT THE GRILL:** PREHEAT YOUR GRILL TO MEDIUM-HIGH HEAT. MAKE SURE IT'S HOT BEFORE YOU START GRILLING TO GET A NICE SEAR ON THE DRUMSTICKS.

- **GRILL THE DRUMSTICKS:** REMOVE THE DRUMSTICKS FROM THE MARINADE (DISCARD THE MARINADE) AND PLACE THEM ON THE GRILL. COOK FOR ABOUT 25-30 MINUTES, TURNING OCCASIONALLY, UNTIL THE DRUMSTICKS ARE GOLDEN BROWN ON THE OUTSIDE AND COOKED THROUGH. THE INTERNAL TEMPERATURE SHOULD REACH 165°F WHEN MEASURED WITH A MEAT THERMOMETER.

- **REST AND SERVE:** LET THE DRUMSTICKS REST FOR A FEW MINUTES AFTER GRILLING TO ALLOW THE JUICES TO REDISTRIBUTE. SERVE HOT.

BBQ GRILLED PULLED PORK

SERVED: 4-6   COOK TIME: 4-5 HOURS   TOTAL TIME: 5,5 HOURS

INGREDIENTS

- 5 TO 7 POUNDS PORK SHOULDER (PORK BUTT)
- 2 TABLESPOONS SALT
- 2 TABLESPOONS BROWN SUGAR
- 2 TABLESPOONS PAPRIKA
- 1 TABLESPOON GARLIC POWDER
- 1 TABLESPOON ONION POWDER
- 1 TEASPOON CAYENNE PEPPER (OPTIONAL FOR EXTRA HEAT)
- 1 TEASPOON BLACK PEPPER
- YOUR FAVORITE BBQ SAUCE FOR BASTING AND SERVING

INSTRUCTIONS

- **PREPARE THE PORK:** RINSE THE PORK SHOULDER AND PAT IT DRY WITH PAPER TOWELS. MIX SALT, BROWN SUGAR, PAPRIKA, GARLIC POWDER, ONION POWDER, CAYENNE, AND BLACK PEPPER IN A BOWL. RUB THE SPICE MIXTURE GENEROUSLY ALL OVER THE PORK, MASSAGING IT INTO THE MEAT.

- **PREHEAT THE BBQ:** PREHEAT YOUR BBQ TO A LOW HEAT SETTING, AROUND 225°F TO 250°F. IF USING CHARCOAL, MAINTAIN A LOW AND STEADY HEAT.

- **GRILL THE PORK:** PLACE THE PORK SHOULDER ON THE COOLER PART OF THE GRILL TO COOK VIA INDIRECT HEAT. COVER THE GRILL. GRILL THE PORK FOR ABOUT 4-5 HOURS, BASTING WITH BBQ SAUCE OCCASIONALLY, UNTIL THE PORK REACHES AN INTERNAL TEMPERATURE OF 195°F TO 205°F. IT SHOULD BE TENDER ENOUGH TO PULL APART.

- **REST AND SERVE:** REMOVE THE PORK FROM THE GRILL AND LET IT REST FOR AT LEAST 20 TO 30 MINUTES. SHRED THE PORK USING TWO FORKS, DISCARDING ANY EXCESS FAT OR GRISTLE. SERVE THE PULLED PORK WITH ADDITIONAL BBQ SAUCE AND YOUR CHOICE OF SIDES LIKE COLESLAW OR ROLLS.

HERB-MARINATED PORK CHOPS

SERVED: 4   COOK TIME: 15 MIN   TOTAL TIME: 2-24 HOURS

INGREDIENTS

FOR THE MARINADE:

- 1/4 CUP OLIVE OIL
- 1/4 CUP SOY SAUCE
- 3 TABLESPOONS LEMON JUICE
- 3 CLOVES GARLIC, MINCED
- 2 TABLESPOONS FRESH ROSEMARY, CHOPPED
- 2 TABLESPOONS FRESH THYME, CHOPPED
- 1 TABLESPOON FRESH SAGE, CHOPPED
- 1 TABLESPOON DIJON MUSTARD
- 1 TEASPOON HONEY
- SALT AND FRESHLY GROUND BLACK PEPPER TO TASTE

FOR THE PORK CHOPS:

- 4 BONE-IN PORK CHOPS, ABOUT 1-INCH THICK

INSTRUCTIONS

- **PREPARE THE MARINADE:** IN A SMALL BOWL, WHISK TOGETHER OLIVE OIL, SOY SAUCE, LEMON JUICE, MINCED GARLIC, CHOPPED ROSEMARY, THYME, SAGE, DIJON MUSTARD, AND HONEY. SEASON WITH SALT AND PEPPER TO TASTE.

- **MARINATE THE PORK CHOPS:** PLACE THE PORK CHOPS IN A LARGE RESEALABLE PLASTIC BAG OR A SHALLOW DISH. POUR THE MARINADE OVER THE PORK CHOPS, MAKING SURE THEY ARE WELL COATED. SEAL THE BAG OR COVER THE DISH. REFRIGERATE AND LET MARINATE FOR AT LEAST 2 HOURS, OR OVERNIGHT FOR MORE PROFOUND FLAVOR.

- **PREHEAT THE GRILL:** PREHEAT YOUR GRILL TO MEDIUM-HIGH HEAT. IF USING A CHARCOAL GRILL, PREPARE FOR DIRECT GRILLING. ENSURE GRATES ARE CLEAN AND LIGHTLY OILED TO PREVENT STICKING.

- **GRILL THE PORK CHOPS:** REMOVE THE PORK CHOPS FROM THE MARINADE, LETTING EXCESS DRIP OFF. DISCARD THE REMAINING MARINADE. GRILL THE PORK CHOPS FOR ABOUT 7-8 MINUTES ON EACH SIDE, OR UNTIL THEY REACH AN INTERNAL TEMPERATURE OF 145°F (63°C). THIS TEMPERATURE ENSURES THE PORK IS COOKED THROUGH YET REMAINS JUICY.

- **REST AND SERVE:** TRANSFER THE GRILLED PORK CHOPS TO A PLATE AND LET THEM REST FOR 5 MINUTES. RESTING ALLOWS THE JUICES TO REDISTRIBUTE THROUGHOUT THE MEAT, MAKING IT MORE TENDER AND FLAVORFUL WHEN SLICED. SERVE WARM WITH YOUR CHOICE OF SIDES.

SWEET AND SPICY PORK RIBS

SERVED: 4-6   COOK TIME: 2-3 HOURS   TOTAL TIME: 3,5 HOURS

INGREDIENTS

- 2 RACKS OF PORK RIBS (ST. LOUIS STYLE OR BABY BACK)
- SALT AND FRESHLY GROUND BLACK PEPPER, TO TASTE

FOR THE RUB:

- ¼ CUP BROWN SUGAR
- 2 TABLESPOONS PAPRIKA
- 1 TABLESPOON GARLIC POWDER
- 1 TABLESPOON ONION POWDER
- 1 TABLESPOON GROUND CUMIN
- 1 TEASPOON CAYENNE PEPPER (ADJUST BASED ON HEAT PREFERENCE)
- 1 TEASPOON CHILI POWDER

FOR THE SAUCE:

- 1 CUP BBQ SAUCE (YOUR CHOICE)
- 2 TABLESPOONS HONEY
- 2 TABLESPOONS APPLE CIDER VINEGAR
- 1 TABLESPOON HOT SAUCE (ADJUST TO TASTE)
- 1 TEASPOON SMOKED PAPRIKA

INSTRUCTIONS

- **PREPARE THE RIBS:** REMOVE THE MEMBRANE FROM THE BACK OF THE RIBS FOR BETTER FLAVOR ABSORPTION. SEASON BOTH SIDES OF THE RIBS WITH SALT AND PEPPER.

- **MAKE THE RUB:** IN A BOWL, COMBINE ALL THE RUB INGREDIENTS. RUB THIS MIXTURE GENEROUSLY OVER BOTH SIDES OF THE RIBS.

- **PREHEAT THE GRILL:** PREHEAT YOUR GRILL TO MEDIUM HEAT, AROUND 300°F. IF USING CHARCOAL, PREPARE FOR INDIRECT GRILLING BY SITUATING THE COALS ON ONE SIDE OF THE GRILL.

- **GRILL THE RIBS:** PLACE THE RIBS ON THE COOLER PART OF THE GRILL (NOT DIRECTLY OVER THE COALS IF USING CHARCOAL). COVER THE GRILL. GRILL THE RIBS FOR ABOUT 2-3 HOURS, TURNING EVERY 30 MINUTES, UNTIL THEY ARE TENDER AND THE MEAT BEGINS TO PULL BACK FROM THE BONES.

- **PREPARE THE SAUCE:** WHILE THE RIBS ARE GRILLING, MIX TOGETHER THE BBQ SAUCE, HONEY, APPLE CIDER VINEGAR, HOT SAUCE, AND SMOKED PAPRIKA IN A SAUCEPAN. HEAT OVER MEDIUM UNTIL IT STARTS TO SIMMER, THEN SET ASIDE.

- **GLAZE THE RIBS:** IN THE LAST 30 MINUTES OF GRILLING, START BASTING THE RIBS WITH THE SAUCE EVERY 10 MINUTES.

- **REST AND SERVE:** REMOVE THE RIBS FROM THE GRILL AND LET THEM REST FOR ABOUT 10 MINUTES BEFORE CUTTING. SERVE WITH EXTRA SAUCE AND YOUR FAVORITE SIDES.

MINTED GRILLED LAMB CHOPS

SERVED: 4 COOK TIME: 6-8 MIN TOTAL TIME: 2-24 HOURS

INGREDIENTS

FOR THE MARINADE:

- 1/2 CUP FRESH MINT LEAVES, FINELY CHOPPED
- 1/4 CUP OLIVE OIL
- 2 TABLESPOONS LEMON JUICE
- 2 GARLIC CLOVES, MINCED
- 1 TEASPOON HONEY
- SALT AND FRESHLY GROUND BLACK PEPPER TO TASTE

FOR THE LAMB CHOPS:

- 8 LAMB CHOPS, ABOUT 1-INCH THICK
- ADDITIONAL FRESH MINT LEAVES FOR GARNISH

INSTRUCTIONS

- **PREPARE THE MARINADE:** IN A BOWL, COMBINE THE CHOPPED MINT, OLIVE OIL, LEMON JUICE, MINCED GARLIC, HONEY, SALT, AND PEPPER. WHISK TOGETHER UNTIL WELL BLENDED.

- **MARINATE THE LAMB CHOPS:** PLACE THE LAMB CHOPS IN A LARGE RESEALABLE PLASTIC BAG OR A SHALLOW DISH. POUR THE MARINADE OVER THE CHOPS, ENSURING THEY ARE ALL EVENLY COATED. SEAL THE BAG OR COVER THE DISH. REFRIGERATE AND LET MARINATE FOR AT LEAST 2 HOURS, OR OVERNIGHT FOR MORE PRONOUNCED FLAVOR.

- **PREHEAT THE GRILL:** PREHEAT YOUR GRILL TO MEDIUM-HIGH HEAT. ENSURE THE GRATES ARE CLEAN AND LIGHTLY OILED TO PREVENT STICKING.

- **GRILL THE LAMB CHOPS:** REMOVE THE LAMB CHOPS FROM THE MARINADE, LETTING EXCESS DRIP OFF. DISCARD THE LEFTOVER MARINADE. GRILL THE CHOPS FOR ABOUT 3-4 MINUTES PER SIDE FOR MEDIUM-RARE, OR ADJUST THE COOKING TIME ACCORDING TO YOUR PREFERENCE. THE INTERNAL TEMPERATURE FOR MEDIUM-RARE SHOULD BE ABOUT 145°F.

- **REST AND SERVE:** TRANSFER THE GRILLED LAMB CHOPS TO A PLATE AND LET THEM REST FOR ABOUT 5 MINUTES. THIS ALLOWS THE JUICES TO REDISTRIBUTE THROUGHOUT THE MEAT, ENHANCING THE FLAVOR AND TENDERNESS. GARNISH WITH ADDITIONAL FRESH MINT LEAVES BEFORE SERVING.

ROSEMARY AND GARLIC LEG OF LAMB

SERVED: 4-6   **COOK TIME: 2 HOURS**   **TOTAL TIME: 2 H 15 M**

INGREDIENTS

- 1 WHOLE LEG OF LAMB (ABOUT 5 TO 7 POUNDS), BONE-IN
- 1/4 CUP OLIVE OIL
- 6 GARLIC CLOVES, MINCED
- 3 TABLESPOONS FRESH ROSEMARY, FINELY CHOPPED
- 2 TABLESPOONS FRESH THYME, FINELY CHOPPED
- ZEST OF 1 LEMON
- 2 TABLESPOONS LEMON JUICE
- SALT AND FRESHLY GROUND BLACK PEPPER, TO TASTE

INSTRUCTIONS

- <u>PREPARE THE MARINADE:</u> IN A SMALL BOWL, MIX THE OLIVE OIL, MINCED GARLIC, CHOPPED ROSEMARY, THYME, LEMON ZEST, AND LEMON JUICE. SEASON GENEROUSLY WITH SALT AND PEPPER.

- <u>MARINATE THE LAMB:</u> MAKE SHALLOW CUTS ACROSS THE LEG OF LAMB WITH A SHARP KNIFE TO HELP THE MARINADE PENETRATE DEEPER INTO THE MEAT. RUB THE MARINADE ALL OVER THE LAMB, ENSURING IT GETS INTO THE CUTS. COVER THE LAMB AND LET IT MARINATE IN THE REFRIGERATOR FOR AT LEAST 4 HOURS, PREFERABLY OVERNIGHT, TO ENHANCE THE FLAVOR AND TENDERNESS.

- <u>PREHEAT THE GRILL:</u> PREHEAT YOUR GRILL TO A MEDIUM SETTING. IF USING CHARCOAL, PREPARE FOR INDIRECT GRILLING BY SITUATING THE COALS ON ONE SIDE OF THE GRILL.

- <u>GRILL THE LAMB:</u> REMOVE THE LAMB FROM THE REFRIGERATOR AT LEAST 30 MINUTES BEFORE COOKING TO ALLOW IT TO COME TO ROOM TEMPERATURE. PLACE THE LAMB ON THE COOLER PART OF THE GRILL (NOT DIRECTLY OVER THE COALS IF USING CHARCOAL) TO COOK MORE EVENLY. COVER AND GRILL, TURNING OCCASIONALLY, UNTIL THE INTERNAL TEMPERATURE REACHES 135°F FOR MEDIUM-RARE OR 145°F FOR MEDIUM, WHICH SHOULD TAKE ABOUT 1.5 TO 2 HOURS DEPENDING ON THE SIZE OF THE LAMB.

- <u>REST AND SERVE:</u> ONCE COOKED, REMOVE THE LAMB FROM THE GRILL AND LET IT REST FOR AT LEAST 20 MINUTES BEFORE CARVING. THIS RESTING PERIOD HELPS THE JUICES REDISTRIBUTE THROUGHOUT THE MEAT, ENSURING A JUICY AND FLAVORFUL MEAL. SLICE THE LAMB AGAINST THE GRAIN AND SERVE.

RACK OF LAMB WITH MUSTARD CRUST

SERVED: 4　　**COOK TIME: 20 MIN**　　**TOTAL TIME: 45 MIN**

INGREDIENTS

- 2 RACKS OF LAMB (ABOUT 1 1/2 POUNDS EACH), TRIMMED AND FRENCHED
- SALT AND FRESHLY GROUND BLACK PEPPER, TO TASTE
- 1/4 CUP DIJON MUSTARD
- 2 TABLESPOONS OLIVE OIL
- 2 CLOVES GARLIC, MINCED
- 1 TABLESPOON FRESH ROSEMARY, FINELY CHOPPED
- 1 TABLESPOON FRESH THYME LEAVES
- 1 CUP BREADCRUMBS, PREFERABLY FRESH
- 2 TABLESPOONS GRATED PARMESAN CHEESE

INSTRUCTIONS

- **PREPARE THE LAMB:** SEASON THE LAMB RACKS THOROUGHLY WITH SALT AND BLACK PEPPER.

- **CREATE THE MUSTARD MIXTURE:** IN A SMALL BOWL, MIX THE DIJON MUSTARD, OLIVE OIL, MINCED GARLIC, CHOPPED ROSEMARY, AND THYME. STIR UNTIL FULLY INCORPORATED.

- **PREPARE THE CRUST:** IN ANOTHER BOWL, MIX THE BREADCRUMBS AND GRATED PARMESAN CHEESE. THIS MIXTURE WILL CREATE THE CRISPY CRUST.

- **APPLY THE MUSTARD MIXTURE:** BRUSH THE MUSTARD MIXTURE GENEROUSLY OVER ALL SIDES OF THE LAMB RACKS, ENSURING THEY ARE WELL COATED.

- **ADD THE BREADCRUMB MIXTURE:** PRESS THE BREADCRUMB MIXTURE ONTO THE MUSTARD-COATED LAMB RACKS, COVERING THEM EVENLY. THE MUSTARD WILL HELP THE BREADCRUMBS ADHERE TO THE MEAT.

- **PREHEAT THE GRILL:** PREHEAT YOUR GRILL TO MEDIUM-HIGH HEAT. MAKE SURE THE GRATES ARE CLEAN AND LIGHTLY OILED.

- **GRILL THE LAMB:** PLACE THE LAMB RACKS ON THE GRILL. COVER AND GRILL FOR ABOUT 20-25 MINUTES, TURNING ONCE HALFWAY THROUGH, OR UNTIL A MEAT THERMOMETER INSERTED INTO THE THICKEST PART OF THE MEAT REGISTERS 135°F FOR MEDIUM-RARE.

- **REST AND SERVE:** LET THE LAMB REST FOR ABOUT 5 MINUTES AFTER REMOVING IT FROM THE GRILL. THIS ALLOWS THE JUICES TO REDISTRIBUTE, MAKING THE MEAT MORE TENDER AND FLAVORFUL WHEN SLICED. SLICE BETWEEN THE RIBS AND SERVE.

FISH
AND
SEAFOOD

GRILLED SALMON WITH LEMON HERB BUTTER

SERVED: 4   COOKING: 10 MIN   TOTAL TIME: 50 MIN

INGREDIENTS

FOR THE SALMON:

- 4 SALMON FILLETS (ABOUT 6 OUNCES EACH), SKIN ON
- 2 TABLESPOONS OLIVE OIL
- SALT AND FRESHLY GROUND BLACK PEPPER TO TASTE

FOR THE LEMON HERB BUTTER:

- 1/2 CUP UNSALTED BUTTER, SOFTENED
- 2 TABLESPOONS FRESH PARSLEY, FINELY CHOPPED
- 1 TABLESPOON FRESH DILL, FINELY CHOPPED
- ZEST OF 1 LEMON
- 2 TABLESPOONS LEMON JUICE
- 1 GARLIC CLOVE, MINCED
- SALT TO TASTE

INSTRUCTIONS

- **PREPARE THE LEMON HERB BUTTER:** IN A SMALL BOWL, COMBINE THE SOFTENED BUTTER, CHOPPED PARSLEY, DILL, LEMON ZEST, LEMON JUICE, AND MINCED GARLIC. MIX UNTIL ALL INGREDIENTS ARE WELL INCORPORATED. SEASON WITH SALT TO TASTE. PLACE THE MIXTURE ON A PIECE OF PLASTIC WRAP AND ROLL INTO A LOG. REFRIGERATE UNTIL FIRM, ABOUT 30 MINUTES.

- **PREHEAT THE GRILL:** PREHEAT YOUR GRILL TO MEDIUM-HIGH HEAT.

- **PREPARE THE SALMON:** PAT THE SALMON FILLETS DRY WITH PAPER TOWELS. BRUSH THEM ON BOTH SIDES WITH OLIVE OIL AND SEASON GENEROUSLY WITH SALT AND PEPPER.

- **GRILL THE SALMON:** PLACE THE SALMON FILLETS SKIN-SIDE DOWN ON THE HOT GRILL. COVER AND COOK FOR 6-8 MINUTES, DEPENDING ON THE THICKNESS OF THE FILLETS. CAREFULLY FLIP THE SALMON AND COOK FOR AN ADDITIONAL 3-4 MINUTES OR UNTIL THE FISH FLAKES EASILY WITH A FORK AND REACHES AN INTERNAL TEMPERATURE OF 145°F.

- **SERVE:** REMOVE THE SALMON FROM THE GRILL AND IMMEDIATELY TOP EACH FILLET WITH A SLICE OF THE CHILLED LEMON HERB BUTTER. ALLOW THE BUTTER TO MELT SLIGHTLY BEFORE SERVING. THE HEAT FROM THE SALMON WILL MELT THE BUTTER, CREATING A RICH AND FLAVORFUL SAUCE.

MEDITERRANEAN GRILLED TUNA STEAKS

SERVED: 4 **COOKING: 8 MIN** **TOTAL TIME: 18 MIN**

INGREDIENTS

- 4 TUNA STEAKS (ABOUT 6 OUNCES EACH, 1 INCH THICK)
- 2 TABLESPOONS OLIVE OIL
- 1 TABLESPOON LEMON ZEST
- 2 TABLESPOONS FRESH LEMON JUICE
- 2 CLOVES GARLIC, MINCED
- 1 TEASPOON DRIED OREGANO
- SALT AND FRESHLY GROUND BLACK PEPPER, TO TASTE
- FRESH HERBS (LIKE PARSLEY OR DILL) FOR GARNISH

INSTRUCTIONS

- **PREPARE THE MARINADE:** IN A SMALL BOWL, MIX THE OLIVE OIL, LEMON ZEST, LEMON JUICE, MINCED GARLIC, AND OREGANO. SEASON WITH SALT AND PEPPER TO TASTE.

- **MARINATE THE TUNA:** PLACE THE TUNA STEAKS IN A DISH OR A RESEALABLE PLASTIC BAG. POUR THE MARINADE OVER THE STEAKS, MAKING SURE EACH PIECE IS WELL-COATED. REFRIGERATE AND LET MARINATE FOR ABOUT 30 MINUTES TO INFUSE THE FLAVORS.

- **PREHEAT THE GRILL:** HEAT YOUR GRILL TO HIGH. MAKE SURE THE GRATES ARE CLEAN AND LIGHTLY OILED.

- **GRILL THE TUNA STEAKS:** REMOVE THE TUNA FROM THE MARINADE, LETTING THE EXCESS DRIP OFF. GRILL THE STEAKS FOR ABOUT 3-4 MINUTES ON EACH SIDE, DEPENDING ON YOUR PREFERRED DONENESS. THE GOAL IS TO ACHIEVE A SLIGHTLY CHARRED EXTERIOR WHILE KEEPING THE CENTER PINK.

- **SERVE:** TRANSFER THE GRILLED TUNA TO PLATES. GARNISH WITH FRESH HERBS AND A SQUEEZE OF LEMON FOR AN EXTRA ZING. OPTIONALLY, DRIZZLE WITH A BIT MORE OLIVE OIL IF DESIRED.

CEDAR PLANKED FISH

SERVED: 4   COOKING: 15 MIN   TOTAL TIME: 25 MIN

INGREDIENTS

- 1 CEDAR PLANK (ABOUT 12 INCHES LONG), SOAKED IN WATER FOR AT LEAST 2 HOURS
- 1 LARGE FISH FILLET (SUCH AS SALMON, TROUT, OR SNAPPER), ABOUT 1 TO 2 POUNDS
- 2 TABLESPOONS OLIVE OIL
- SALT AND FRESHLY GROUND BLACK PEPPER
- 2 TABLESPOONS FRESH DILL, CHOPPED, OR OTHER PREFERRED HERBS (SUCH AS PARSLEY OR THYME)
- 1 LEMON, THINLY SLICED
- OPTIONAL: 1 GARLIC CLOVE, MINCED

INSTRUCTIONS

- **PREPARE THE CEDAR PLANK:** SOAK THE CEDAR PLANK IN WATER FOR AT LEAST 2 HOURS TO PREVENT IT FROM BURNING DURING THE GRILLING PROCESS. YOU CAN USE A WEIGHT TO KEEP IT SUBMERGED.

- **PREPARE THE FISH:** RINSE THE FISH FILLET UNDER COLD WATER AND PAT DRY WITH PAPER TOWELS. BRUSH THE FILLET WITH OLIVE OIL ON BOTH SIDES. SEASON GENEROUSLY WITH SALT, PEPPER, AND MINCED GARLIC (IF USING). SPRINKLE CHOPPED DILL OR OTHER HERBS OVER THE FISH. ARRANGE THE LEMON SLICES ON TOP OF THE FILLET.

- **PREHEAT THE GRILL:** PREHEAT YOUR GRILL TO MEDIUM-HIGH HEAT.

- **GRILL THE FISH ON THE PLANK:** PLACE THE SOAKED CEDAR PLANK ON THE GRILL FOR ABOUT 3-5 MINUTES UNTIL IT STARTS TO SMOKE AND CHAR SLIGHTLY. PLACE THE PREPARED FISH FILLET ON THE PLANK. CLOSE THE GRILL LID TO ALLOW THE SMOKE TO ENVELOP THE FISH. COOK FOR ABOUT 12-15 MINUTES OR UNTIL THE FISH IS OPAQUE AND FLAKES EASILY WITH A FORK. THE EXACT TIME WILL DEPEND ON THE THICKNESS OF THE FILLET.

- **SERVE IMMEDIATELY:** CAREFULLY REMOVE THE PLANK FROM THE GRILL. THE PLANK WILL BE HOT, SO USE GLOVES OR A SPATULA. SERVE THE FISH DIRECTLY FROM THE PLANK FOR A RUSTIC PRESENTATION, OR TRANSFER IT TO A SERVING PLATTER.

FISH TACOS WITH MANGO SALSA

SERVED: 4   COOKING: 6-8 MIN   TOTAL TIME: 30 MIN

INGREDIENTS

FOR THE FISH:

- 1 POUND FIRM WHITE FISH FILLETS (LIKE COD, HALIBUT, OR MAHI-MAHI)
- 2 TABLESPOONS OLIVE OIL
- 1 TEASPOON CHILI POWDER
- 1 TEASPOON PAPRIKA
- 1/2 TEASPOON GROUND CUMIN
- SALT AND FRESHLY GROUND BLACK PEPPER TO TASTE
- 8 SMALL CORN OR FLOUR TORTILLAS

FOR THE MANGO SALSA:

- 1 RIPE MANGO, PEELED AND DICED
- 1/4 CUP RED BELL PEPPER, FINELY CHOPPED
- 1/4 CUP RED ONION, FINELY CHOPPED
- 1 SMALL JALAPEÑO, SEEDED AND MINCED (ADJUST BASED ON HEAT PREFERENCE)
- JUICE OF 1 LIME
- 1/4 CUP FRESH CILANTRO, CHOPPED
- SALT TO TASTE

INSTRUCTIONS

- **PREPARE THE MANGO SALSA:** IN A MEDIUM BOWL, COMBINE THE DICED MANGO, RED BELL PEPPER, RED ONION, JALAPEÑO, LIME JUICE, AND CILANTRO. MIX WELL. SEASON WITH SALT TO TASTE AND SET ASIDE TO LET THE FLAVORS MELD.

- **SEASON THE FISH:** PAT THE FISH FILLETS DRY WITH PAPER TOWELS. IN A SMALL BOWL, MIX TOGETHER THE OLIVE OIL, CHILI POWDER, PAPRIKA, CUMIN, SALT, AND PEPPER. RUB THIS SPICE MIXTURE ALL OVER THE FISH FILLETS, COATING THEM EVENLY.

- **COOK THE FISH:** HEAT A GRILL PAN OR SKILLET OVER MEDIUM-HIGH HEAT. WHEN HOT, ADD THE SEASONED FISH FILLETS. COOK FOR ABOUT 3-4 MINUTES PER SIDE OR UNTIL THE FISH IS OPAQUE AND FLAKES EASILY WITH A FORK. REMOVE FROM HEAT AND LET REST FOR A FEW MINUTES. BREAK THE FISH INTO CHUNKS OR SHRED IT LIGHTLY WITH A FORK.

- **WARM THE TORTILLAS:** HEAT THE TORTILLAS IN A DRY SKILLET OVER MEDIUM-HIGH HEAT FOR ABOUT 30 SECONDS ON EACH SIDE, OR DIRECTLY OVER THE FLAME FOR A CHARRED EFFECT.

- **ASSEMBLE THE TACOS:** SPOON SOME OF THE FISH ONTO EACH WARMED TORTILLA. TOP WITH A GENEROUS AMOUNT OF MANGO SALSA.

- **SERVE:** SERVE THE FISH TACOS IMMEDIATELY, WITH LIME WEDGES ON THE SIDE FOR EXTRA ZEST IF DESIRED.

BEER-STEAMED MUSSELS

SERVED: 4-6   COOKING: 15 MIN   TOTAL TIME: 30 MIN

INGREDIENTS

- 2 POUNDS FRESH MUSSELS, CLEANED AND DEBEARDED
- 1 CUP BEER (LIGHT ALE OR LAGER WORKS BEST)
- 2 TABLESPOONS BUTTER
- 2 GARLIC CLOVES, MINCED
- 1 SMALL ONION, FINELY CHOPPED
- 1/2 TEASPOON RED PEPPER FLAKES (OPTIONAL, FOR A BIT OF HEAT)
- FRESH PARSLEY, CHOPPED (FOR GARNISH)
- SALT AND FRESHLY GROUND BLACK PEPPER, TO TASTE
- CRUSTY BREAD, FOR SERVING

INSTRUCTIONS

- **PREPARE THE MUSSELS:** RINSE THE MUSSELS UNDER COLD WATER. REMOVE ANY BEARDS AND SCRAPE OFF BARNACLES. DISCARD ANY MUSSELS THAT DON'T CLOSE WHEN TAPPED.

- **PREPARE THE FOIL PACKET:** LAY OUT A LARGE PIECE OF HEAVY-DUTY ALUMINUM FOIL, ENOUGH TO FOLD OVER AND SEAL THE MUSSELS INSIDE. PLACE THE CLEANED MUSSELS IN THE CENTER OF THE FOIL. SCATTER THE MINCED GARLIC, CHOPPED ONION, AND OPTIONAL RED PEPPER FLAKES OVER THE MUSSELS. DOT WITH PIECES OF BUTTER AND POUR THE BEER OVER THE MUSSELS. SEASON WITH SALT AND PEPPER. FOLD THE FOIL OVER THE MUSSELS AND CRIMP THE EDGES TO SEAL TIGHTLY, MAKING SURE THERE IS SOME SPACE INSIDE FOR STEAM TO CIRCULATE.

- **GRILL THE MUSSELS:** PREHEAT THE GRILL TO MEDIUM-HIGH HEAT. PLACE THE FOIL PACKET DIRECTLY ON THE GRILL. CLOSE THE LID OF THE GRILL TO KEEP THE HEAT IN. COOK FOR ABOUT 10-15 MINUTES, OR UNTIL ALL THE MUSSELS HAVE OPENED. DISCARD ANY THAT REMAIN CLOSED.

- **SERVE:** CAREFULLY OPEN THE FOIL PACKET (WATCH OUT FOR HOT STEAM). TRANSFER THE MUSSELS AND THEIR JUICES TO A LARGE BOWL. GARNISH WITH CHOPPED FRESH PARSLEY. SERVE IMMEDIATELY WITH CRUSTY BREAD TO SOAK UP THE FLAVORFUL BROTH.

GARLIC BUTTER SHRIMP SKEWERS

SERVED: 4   COOKING: 6 MIN   TOTAL TIME: 26 MIN

INGREDIENTS

- 1 POUND LARGE SHRIMP, PEELED AND DEVEINED (TAILS LEFT ON)
- 4 TABLESPOONS UNSALTED BUTTER
- 3 CLOVES GARLIC, MINCED
- 1 TABLESPOON FRESH PARSLEY, FINELY CHOPPED
- JUICE OF 1 LEMON
- SALT AND FRESHLY GROUND BLACK PEPPER, TO TASTE
- OPTIONAL: RED PEPPER FLAKES FOR A SPICY KICK
- WOODEN OR METAL SKEWERS (IF USING WOODEN SKEWERS, SOAK THEM IN WATER FOR 30 MINUTES BEFORE GRILLING TO PREVENT BURNING)

INSTRUCTIONS

- **PREPARE THE GARLIC BUTTER:** IN A SMALL SAUCEPAN, MELT THE BUTTER OVER MEDIUM HEAT. ADD THE MINCED GARLIC AND COOK FOR 1-2 MINUTES UNTIL FRAGRANT BUT NOT BROWNED. REMOVE FROM HEAT AND STIR IN THE FRESH PARSLEY, LEMON JUICE, AND RED PEPPER FLAKES (IF USING). SET ASIDE SOME OF THE MIXTURE FOR SERVING AND KEEP THE REST FOR BASTING.

- **PREPARE THE SHRIMP:** RINSE THE SHRIMP AND PAT THEM DRY WITH PAPER TOWELS. SEASON THE SHRIMP WITH SALT AND BLACK PEPPER.

- **ASSEMBLE THE SKEWERS:** THREAD THE SHRIMP ONTO THE SKEWERS, PIERCING THROUGH THE HEAD AND TAIL TO SECURE THEM.

- **PREHEAT THE GRILL:** PREHEAT YOUR GRILL TO MEDIUM-HIGH HEAT.

- **GRILL THE SHRIMP:** PLACE THE SHRIMP SKEWERS ON THE HOT GRILL. GRILL FOR ABOUT 2-3 MINUTES ON EACH SIDE, BASTING FREQUENTLY WITH THE GARLIC BUTTER MIXTURE. THE SHRIMP ARE DONE WHEN THEY TURN PINK AND OPAQUE.

- **SERVE:** ONCE COOKED, REMOVE THE SKEWERS FROM THE GRILL. DRIZZLE WITH THE RESERVED GARLIC BUTTER MIXTURE BEFORE SERVING.

GRILLED LOBSTER WITH HERB BUTTER

SERVED: 4   COOKING: 10 MIN   TOTAL TIME: 30 MIN

INGREDIENTS

- 2 WHOLE LIVE LOBSTERS (ABOUT 1.5 POUNDS EACH)
- 1/2 CUP UNSALTED BUTTER, SOFTENED
- 2 TABLESPOONS FRESH PARSLEY, FINELY CHOPPED
- 1 TABLESPOON FRESH TARRAGON, FINELY CHOPPED
- 1 TABLESPOON FRESH CHIVES, FINELY CHOPPED
- 2 CLOVES GARLIC, MINCED
- ZEST OF 1 LEMON
- SALT AND FRESHLY GROUND BLACK PEPPER, TO TASTE
- LEMON WEDGES, FOR SERVING

INSTRUCTIONS

- **PREPARE THE HERB BUTTER:** IN A SMALL BOWL, MIX TOGETHER THE SOFTENED BUTTER, CHOPPED PARSLEY, TARRAGON, CHIVES, MINCED GARLIC, AND LEMON ZEST. SEASON WITH SALT AND PEPPER TO TASTE. SET ASIDE SOME OF THE BUTTER FOR SERVING AND KEEP THE REST FOR BASTING WHILE GRILLING.

- **PREHEAT THE GRILL:** PREHEAT YOUR GRILL TO MEDIUM-HIGH HEAT.

- **PREPARE THE LOBSTERS:** BRING A LARGE POT OF SALTED WATER TO A BOIL. BLANCH THE LOBSTERS BY BOILING THEM FOR ABOUT 2 MINUTES. REMOVE AND LET COOL SLIGHTLY. USING A LARGE CHEF'S KNIFE, SPLIT THE LOBSTERS IN HALF LENGTHWISE. REMOVE ANY INNARDS AND THE VEIN RUNNING DOWN THE TAIL. CRACK THE CLAWS SLIGHTLY USING A NUTCRACKER TO MAKE THEM EASIER TO EAT AFTER GRILLING.

- **GRILL THE LOBSTERS:** BRUSH THE CUT SIDES OF THE LOBSTERS WITH SOME OF THE HERB BUTTER. PLACE THE LOBSTERS ON THE GRILL, SHELL SIDE DOWN, AND COOK FOR ABOUT 5-7 MINUTES. FLIP THE LOBSTERS TO CUT-SIDE DOWN, BASTE AGAIN WITH THE HERB BUTTER, AND GRILL FOR ANOTHER 4-5 MINUTES, OR UNTIL THE LOBSTER MEAT IS FIRM AND OPAQUE.

- **SERVE:** SERVE THE GRILLED LOBSTERS IMMEDIATELY, TOPPED WITH DOLLOPS OF THE RESERVED HERB BUTTER AND ACCOMPANIED BY LEMON WEDGES.

SEARED SCALLOPS WITH BALSAMIC REDUCTION

SERVED: 4   COOKING: 6 MIN   TOTAL TIME: 30 MIN

INGREDIENTS

- 1 POUND LARGE SEA SCALLOPS, SIDE MUSCLE REMOVED
- SALT AND FRESHLY GROUND BLACK PEPPER
- 2 TABLESPOONS OLIVE OIL
- 1 TABLESPOON UNSALTED BUTTER (FOR FINISHING)

FOR THE BALSAMIC REDUCTION:
- 1 CUP BALSAMIC VINEGAR
- 2 TABLESPOONS BROWN SUGAR (OPTIONAL, FOR ADDED SWEETNESS)

INSTRUCTIONS

- **PREPARE THE BALSAMIC REDUCTION:** IN A SMALL SAUCEPAN OVER MEDIUM HEAT, COMBINE THE BALSAMIC VINEGAR AND BROWN SUGAR (IF USING). BRING THE MIXTURE TO A BOIL, THEN REDUCE THE HEAT AND SIMMER UNTIL THE VINEGAR THICKENS AND REDUCES TO ABOUT A QUARTER OF ITS ORIGINAL VOLUME, APPROXIMATELY 15-20 MINUTES. THE REDUCTION SHOULD COAT THE BACK OF A SPOON. SET ASIDE AND KEEP WARM.

- **PREPARE THE SCALLOPS:** PAT THE SCALLOPS DRY WITH PAPER TOWELS AND SEASON BOTH SIDES WITH SALT AND PEPPER.

- **PREHEAT THE GRILL:** PREHEAT YOUR GRILL TO MEDIUM-HIGH HEAT. ENSURE THE GRATES ARE CLEAN AND LIGHTLY OILED TO PREVENT STICKING.

- **GRILL THE SCALLOPS:** BRUSH THE SCALLOPS WITH OLIVE OIL AND PLACE THEM ON THE HOT GRILL. GRILL FOR ABOUT 2-3 MINUTES ON EACH SIDE, OR UNTIL THE SCALLOPS DEVELOP A GOLDEN CRUST AND ARE COOKED THROUGH (OPAQUE).

- **FINISH WITH BUTTER:** AFTER TURNING THE SCALLOPS, ADD A SMALL PIECE OF BUTTER ATOP EACH SCALLOP WHILE THE SECOND SIDE FINISHES COOKING. THIS WILL ADD A RICH FINISH TO THE SCALLOPS.

- **SERVE:** ARRANGE THE GRILLED SCALLOPS ON PLATES AND DRIZZLE WITH THE WARM BALSAMIC REDUCTION. OPTIONALLY, YOU CAN GARNISH WITH FRESH HERBS LIKE BASIL OR PARSLEY FOR ADDITIONAL FLAVOR AND A POP OF COLOR.

GRILLED OCTOPUS WITH OLIVE OIL AND LEMON

INGREDIENTS

- 1 WHOLE OCTOPUS, CLEANED (ABOUT 2-3 POUNDS)
- 1/4 CUP OLIVE OIL, PLUS MORE FOR DRIZZLING
- 2 LEMONS, ONE SLICED AND ONE FOR JUICING
- 4 CLOVES GARLIC, SMASHED
- 1 BAY LEAF
- SALT AND FRESHLY GROUND BLACK PEPPER
- FRESH PARSLEY, CHOPPED (FOR GARNISH)

INSTRUCTIONS

- **PREPARE THE OCTOPUS:** IF NOT ALREADY DONE, CLEAN THE OCTOPUS BY REMOVING THE BEAK AND INK SAC AND RINSING UNDER COLD WATER. IN A LARGE POT, COMBINE THE OCTOPUS, A SLICED LEMON, GARLIC, AND BAY LEAF. COVER WITH WATER. BRING TO A BOIL, THEN REDUCE TO A SIMMER. COOK FOR ABOUT 45-60 MINUTES UNTIL THE OCTOPUS IS TENDER WHEN PIERCED WITH A FORK.

- **COOL AND MARINATE:** REMOVE THE OCTOPUS FROM THE POT AND LET IT COOL SLIGHTLY. ONCE COOL ENOUGH TO HANDLE, CUT THE OCTOPUS INTO PIECES (TENTACLES AND BODY) SUITABLE FOR GRILLING. TOSS THE OCTOPUS PIECES WITH OLIVE OIL, LEMON JUICE, SALT, AND PEPPER. LET MARINATE FOR AT LEAST 30 MINUTES.

- **PREHEAT THE GRILL:** PREHEAT YOUR GRILL TO MEDIUM-HIGH HEAT. ENSURE THE GRATES ARE CLEAN AND LIGHTLY OILED.

- **GRILL THE OCTOPUS:** PLACE THE OCTOPUS PIECES ON THE HOT GRILL. GRILL FOR ABOUT 4-6 MINUTES ON EACH SIDE, OR UNTIL THE OCTOPUS HAS CHARRED MARKS AND IS HEATED THROUGH.

- **SERVE:** ARRANGE THE GRILLED OCTOPUS ON A SERVING PLATTER. DRIZZLE WITH MORE OLIVE OIL AND A SQUEEZE OF FRESH LEMON JUICE. GARNISH WITH CHOPPED PARSLEY AND ADDITIONAL LEMON SLICES.

SPICY GRILLED SQUID WITH LEMON BASIL

SERVED: 4   COOKING: 4-6 MIN   TOTAL TIME: 1 HOUR

INGREDIENTS

- 11 LB FRESH SQUID, CLEANED AND BODIES CUT INTO RINGS, TENTACLES LEFT WHOLE
- 3 TABLESPOONS EXTRA VIRGIN OLIVE OIL
- 2 TABLESPOONS FRESH BASIL, CHOPPED
- 2 TABLESPOONS SUNDRIED TOMATOES, FINELY CHOPPED
- 1 CLOVE GARLIC, MINCED
- JUICE OF 1 LEMON
- SALT AND FRESHLY GROUND BLACK PEPPER, TO TASTE
- 1 TEASPOON CRUSHED RED PEPPER FLAKES (OPTIONAL, FOR A SPICY TOUCH)

INSTRUCTIONS

- **PREPARE THE MARINADE:** IN A MIXING BOWL, COMBINE OLIVE OIL, CHOPPED BASIL, SUNDRIED TOMATOES, MINCED GARLIC, LEMON JUICE, SALT, BLACK PEPPER, AND RED PEPPER FLAKES. STIR TO BLEND ALL THE INGREDIENTS TOGETHER.

- **MARINATE THE SQUID:** PLACE THE SQUID IN A LARGE RESEALABLE PLASTIC BAG OR A SHALLOW BOWL. POUR THE MARINADE OVER THE SQUID, ENSURING EACH PIECE IS EVENLY COATED. REFRIGERATE FOR 30 MINUTES TO ALLOW THE FLAVORS TO MELD.

- **PREHEAT THE GRILL:** PREHEAT YOUR GRILL TO MEDIUM-HIGH HEAT. CLEAN THE GRILL GRATES AND LIGHTLY OIL THEM TO PREVENT STICKING.

- **GRILL THE SQUID:** REMOVE THE SQUID FROM THE MARINADE AND SHAKE OFF EXCESS. GRILL THE SQUID FOR ABOUT 2-3 MINUTES ON EACH SIDE OR UNTIL THEY ARE TENDER AND HAVE SLIGHT CHAR MARKS.

- **SERVE:** ARRANGE THE GRILLED SQUID ON A PLATTER. DRIZZLE WITH A LITTLE MORE OLIVE OIL AND A SQUEEZE OF FRESH LEMON JUICE. GARNISH WITH ADDITIONAL CHOPPED BASIL.

GRILLED TUNA STEAKS WITH AVOCADO SALSA

SERVED: 4   COOKING: 4-6 MIN   TOTAL TIME: 20 MIN

INGREDIENTS

- 4 TUNA STEAKS (ABOUT 6 OUNCES EACH)
- 2 TABLESPOONS OLIVE OIL
- SALT AND FRESHLY GROUND BLACK PEPPER, TO TASTE

FOR THE AVOCADO SALSA:

- 1 RIPE AVOCADO, DICED
- 1 SMALL RED ONION, FINELY CHOPPED
- 1 JALAPEÑO, SEEDED AND FINELY CHOPPED
- JUICE OF 1 LIME
- 2 TABLESPOONS CHOPPED FRESH CILANTRO
- SALT AND PEPPER, TO TASTE

INSTRUCTIONS

- <u>PREPARE THE AVOCADO SALSA:</u> IN A MEDIUM BOWL, COMBINE THE DICED AVOCADO, RED ONION, JALAPEÑO, LIME JUICE, AND CILANTRO. SEASON WITH SALT AND PEPPER TO TASTE. MIX GENTLY AND SET ASIDE TO LET THE FLAVORS MELD.

- <u>PREPARE THE TUNA STEAKS:</u> PREHEAT YOUR GRILL TO HIGH HEAT. BRUSH THE TUNA STEAKS LIGHTLY WITH OLIVE OIL AND SEASON WITH SALT AND PEPPER ON BOTH SIDES.

- <u>GRILL THE TUNA:</u> PLACE THE TUNA STEAKS ON THE HOT GRILL. GRILL FOR ABOUT 2-3 MINUTES ON EACH SIDE FOR MEDIUM-RARE, OR ADJUST THE COOKING TIME BASED ON YOUR PREFERENCE FOR DONENESS.

- <u>SERVE:</u> SERVE THE GRILLED TUNA STEAKS IMMEDIATELY, TOPPED WITH A GENEROUS SPOONFUL OF AVOCADO SALSA.

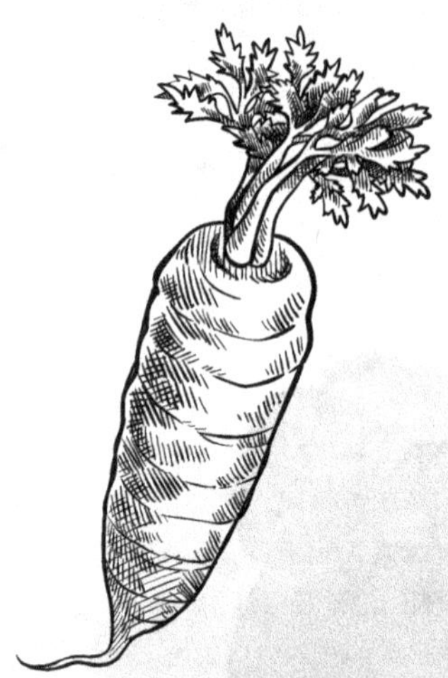

VEGETABLES

GRILLED ASPARAGUS WITH LEMON ZEST

SERVED: 4   COOKING: 6 MIN   TOTAL TIME: 18 MIN

INGREDIENTS

- 1 POUND FRESH ASPARAGUS
- 2 TABLESPOONS OLIVE OIL
- SALT AND FRESHLY GROUND BLACK PEPPER TO TASTE
- ZEST OF 1 LEMON
- OPTIONAL: GRATED PARMESAN CHEESE OR A SQUEEZE OF FRESH LEMON JUICE FOR SERVING

INSTRUCTIONS

- **PREPARE THE ASPARAGUS:** RINSE THE ASPARAGUS AND TRIM OFF THE TOUGH BOTTOM ENDS. TO FIND THE NATURAL BREAKING POINT, YOU CAN BEND ONE SPEAR UNTIL IT SNAPS AND THEN CUT THE REST TO MATCH.

- **SEASON THE ASPARAGUS:** PLACE THE ASPARAGUS ON A TRAY OR IN A LARGE BOWL. DRIZZLE WITH OLIVE OIL AND TOSS TO COAT EACH SPEAR EVENLY. SEASON GENEROUSLY WITH SALT AND FRESHLY GROUND BLACK PEPPER.

- **PREHEAT THE GRILL:** PREHEAT YOUR GRILL TO MEDIUM-HIGH HEAT. ENSURE THE GRATES ARE CLEAN TO PREVENT STICKING.

- **GRILL THE ASPARAGUS:** ARRANGE THE ASPARAGUS SPEARS PERPENDICULAR TO THE GRILL GRATES TO PREVENT THEM FROM FALLING THROUGH. GRILL THE ASPARAGUS FOR ABOUT 6-8 MINUTES, TURNING OCCASIONALLY, UNTIL THEY ARE TENDER AND CHARRED IN SPOTS.

- **ADD LEMON ZEST:** ONCE THE ASPARAGUS IS OFF THE GRILL, IMMEDIATELY ZEST THE LEMON OVER THE HOT ASPARAGUS. THE HEAT WILL HELP RELEASE THE AROMATIC OILS FROM THE ZEST, ENHANCING THE FLAVOR.

- **SERVE:** TRANSFER THE GRILLED ASPARAGUS TO A SERVING PLATTER. IF DESIRED, ADD A SPRINKLE OF GRATED PARMESAN CHEESE OR A SQUEEZE OF FRESH LEMON JUICE FOR EXTRA FLAVOR. SERVE IMMEDIATELY WHILE WARM AND CRISP.

CHARRED CORN ON THE COB WITH HERB BUTTER

SERVED: 4   COOKING: 10 MIN   TOTAL TIME: 25 MIN

INGREDIENTS

- 4 EARS OF CORN, HUSKS AND SILKS REMOVED
- OLIVE OIL, FOR BRUSHING
- SALT AND FRESHLY GROUND BLACK PEPPER, TO TASTE

FOR THE HERB BUTTER:

- 1/2 CUP UNSALTED BUTTER, SOFTENED
- 2 TABLESPOONS FRESH PARSLEY, FINELY CHOPPED
- 1 TABLESPOON FRESH BASIL, FINELY CHOPPED
- 1 TABLESPOON FRESH CHIVES, FINELY CHOPPED
- 1 GARLIC CLOVE, MINCED
- SALT AND FRESHLY GROUND BLACK PEPPER, TO TASTE
- OPTIONAL: PINCH OF CHILI FLAKES FOR A BIT OF HEAT

INSTRUCTIONS

- **PREPARE THE HERB BUTTER:** IN A SMALL BOWL, MIX TOGETHER THE SOFTENED BUTTER, CHOPPED PARSLEY, BASIL, CHIVES, MINCED GARLIC, AND OPTIONAL CHILI FLAKES IF USING. SEASON WITH SALT AND PEPPER TO TASTE. PLACE THE MIXED HERB BUTTER ON A PIECE OF PLASTIC WRAP AND ROLL INTO A LOG. TWIST THE ENDS TO SEAL AND REFRIGERATE UNTIL FIRM.

- **PREHEAT THE GRILL:** PREHEAT YOUR GRILL TO MEDIUM-HIGH HEAT. ENSURE THE GRILL GRATES ARE CLEAN TO PREVENT STICKING.

- **PREPARE THE CORN:** BRUSH EACH EAR OF CORN LIGHTLY WITH OLIVE OIL AND SEASON WITH SALT AND PEPPER.

- **GRILL THE CORN:** PLACE THE CORN DIRECTLY ON THE GRILL GRATES. GRILL THE CORN, TURNING OCCASIONALLY, UNTIL IT IS TENDER AND CHARRED IN SPOTS, ABOUT 10-12 MINUTES.

- **SERVE:** ONCE THE CORN IS GRILLED, REMOVE IT FROM THE GRILL AND IMMEDIATELY APPLY SLICES OF THE CHILLED HERB BUTTER OVER THE HOT CORN SO THE BUTTER MELTS AND COATS EACH COB. SERVE THE CORN WARM, ENSURING EACH PIECE HAS A GENEROUS AMOUNT OF MELTED HERB BUTTER.

SMOKEY GRILLED EGGPLANT SLICES

SERVED: 4-6   PREP TIME: 40 MIN   TOTAL TIME: 50 MIN

INGREDIENTS

- 2 LARGE EGGPLANTS
- OLIVE OIL, FOR BRUSHING
- SALT AND FRESHLY GROUND BLACK PEPPER, TO TASTE
- OPTIONAL: SMOKED PAPRIKA OR CUMIN FOR EXTRA SMOKINESS

INSTRUCTIONS

- **PREPARE THE EGGPLANT:** SLICE THE EGGPLANTS INTO ROUNDS OR LENGTHWISE INTO 1/2-INCH THICK SLICES. SALT THE SLICES LIBERALLY AND LET THEM SIT IN A COLANDER FOR ABOUT 30 MINUTES TO DRAW OUT MOISTURE. THIS HELPS TO REDUCE BITTERNESS AND IMPROVES TEXTURE. RINSE THE SLICES UNDER COLD WATER, THEN PAT DRY WITH PAPER TOWELS.

- **SEASON THE EGGPLANT:** BRUSH EACH SLICE GENEROUSLY ON BOTH SIDES WITH OLIVE OIL. SEASON WITH SALT, FRESHLY GROUND BLACK PEPPER, AND SMOKED PAPRIKA OR CUMIN IF USING.

- **PREHEAT THE GRILL:** PREHEAT YOUR GRILL TO MEDIUM-HIGH HEAT. ENSURE THE GRATES ARE CLEAN AND LIGHTLY OILED TO PREVENT STICKING.

- **GRILL THE EGGPLANT:** PLACE THE EGGPLANT SLICES ON THE GRILL. COOK FOR 4-5 MINUTES ON EACH SIDE, OR UNTIL THE SLICES ARE TENDER AND MARKED WITH GRILL LINES. IF THE EGGPLANT STARTS TO DRY OUT OR BURN, BRUSH ON MORE OLIVE OIL AS NEEDED.

- **SERVE:** TRANSFER THE GRILLED EGGPLANT SLICES TO A SERVING PLATTER. THEY CAN BE SERVED HOT OR AT ROOM TEMPERATURE. OPTIONAL GARNISHES INCLUDE A DRIZZLE OF BALSAMIC GLAZE, A SPRINKLE OF FRESH HERBS (SUCH AS BASIL OR PARSLEY), OR A DOLLOP OF YOGURT OR TAHINI SAUCE.

JALAPEÑO POPPERS STUFFED WITH CREAM CHEESE AND WRAPPED IN BACON

SERVED: 24 POPPERS   **PREP TIME: 20 MIN**   **TOTAL TIME: 35-45 MIN**

INGREDIENTS

- 12 JALAPEÑO PEPPERS
- 1 PACKAGE (8 OZ) CREAM CHEESE, SOFTENED
- 1 CUP SHREDDED CHEDDAR CHEESE
- 1/2 TEASPOON GARLIC POWDER
- 1/4 TEASPOON SALT
- 1/4 TEASPOON BLACK PEPPER
- 12 SLICES BACON, CUT IN HALF
- TOOTHPICKS

INSTRUCTIONS

- **PREPARE THE JALAPEÑOS:** SLICE EACH JALAPEÑO IN HALF LENGTHWISE. USING A SPOON, CAREFULLY REMOVE THE SEEDS AND VEINS FROM EACH HALF. IF YOU PREFER LESS HEAT, ENSURE ALL SEEDS ARE REMOVED AS THEY CONTAIN MUCH OF THE PEPPER'S SPICINESS.

- **MAKE THE FILLING:** IN A MIXING BOWL, COMBINE THE SOFTENED CREAM CHEESE, SHREDDED CHEDDAR CHEESE, GARLIC POWDER, SALT, AND BLACK PEPPER. MIX UNTIL WELL BLENDED.

- **STUFF THE JALAPEÑOS:** SPOON THE CHEESE MIXTURE INTO EACH JALAPEÑO HALF, FILLING THEM GENEROUSLY.

- **WRAP WITH BACON:** WRAP A HALF SLICE OF BACON AROUND EACH STUFFED JALAPEÑO HALF. SECURE THE BACON WITH A TOOTHPICK TO ENSURE IT STAYS IN PLACE DURING COOKING.

- **PREHEAT THE GRILL:** PREHEAT YOUR GRILL TO MEDIUM-HIGH HEAT.

- **COOK THE POPPERS:** PLACE THE BACON-WRAPPED JALAPEÑOS ON THE GRILL OVER INDIRECT HEAT. GRILL FOR ABOUT 15-20 MINUTES, TURNING OCCASIONALLY, UNTIL THE BACON IS CRISPY AND THE PEPPERS ARE TENDER.

- **SERVE:** LET THE JALAPEÑO POPPERS COOL SLIGHTLY BEFORE SERVING, AS THE FILLING CAN BE VERY HOT. SERVE THEM WARM AS A TASTY APPETIZER.

SPICED CAULIFLOWER STEAKS

SERVED: 2-4 PREP TIME: 10 MIN TOTAL TIME: 20-35 MIN

INGREDIENTS

- 1 LARGE HEAD OF CAULIFLOWER
- 3 TABLESPOONS OLIVE OIL
- 1 TEASPOON PAPRIKA
- 1 TEASPOON GARLIC POWDER
- 1/2 TEASPOON CUMIN
- 1/2 TEASPOON CORIANDER
- SALT AND FRESHLY GROUND BLACK PEPPER, TO TASTE
- FRESH PARSLEY OR CILANTRO, CHOPPED (FOR GARNISH)
- LEMON WEDGES, FOR SERVING

INSTRUCTIONS

- <u>PREPARE THE CAULIFLOWER:</u> REMOVE THE LEAVES AND TRIM THE STEM OF THE CAULIFLOWER, KEEPING THE CORE INTACT. PLACE THE CAULIFLOWER WITH ITS BASE ON A CUTTING BOARD. USING A LARGE KNIFE, SLICE THE CAULIFLOWER INTO APPROXIMATELY 1/2-INCH THICK STEAKS FROM THE CENTER PART. YOU MAY GET 2-4 GOOD STEAKS FROM A LARGE HEAD, PLUS SOME FLORETS FROM THE SIDES.

- <u>MAKE THE SPICE MIX:</u> IN A SMALL BOWL, COMBINE THE OLIVE OIL, PAPRIKA, GARLIC POWDER, CUMIN, CORIANDER, SALT, AND BLACK PEPPER. MIX WELL TO CREATE A SPICED OIL.

- <u>SEASON THE CAULIFLOWER:</u> BRUSH BOTH SIDES OF EACH CAULIFLOWER STEAK WITH THE SPICED OIL. MAKE SURE TO USE IT GENEROUSLY TO COAT WELL.

- <u>COOK THE CAULIFLOWER STEAKS:</u>
  - <u>GRILL METHOD:</u> PREHEAT THE GRILL TO MEDIUM-HIGH HEAT. PLACE THE CAULIFLOWER STEAKS DIRECTLY ON THE GRILL. COOK FOR 5-6 MINUTES PER SIDE OR UNTIL THEY ARE GOLDEN AND TENDER, WITH NICE CHAR MARKS.
  - <u>OVEN METHOD:</u> PREHEAT THE OVEN TO 400°F (200°C). PLACE THE CAULIFLOWER STEAKS ON A BAKING SHEET LINED WITH PARCHMENT PAPER. BAKE FOR ABOUT 20-25 MINUTES, FLIPPING HALFWAY THROUGH, UNTIL GOLDEN AND TENDER.

- <u>SERVE:</u> TRANSFER THE COOKED CAULIFLOWER STEAKS TO A SERVING PLATTER. GARNISH WITH CHOPPED PARSLEY OR CILANTRO, AND SERVE WITH LEMON WEDGES ON THE SIDE.

GRILLED STUFFED BELL PEPPERS

SERVED: 4　　**PREP TIME: 20 MIN**　　**COOKING: 20 MIN**　　**TOTAL TIME: 40 MIN**

INGREDIENTS

- 4 LARGE BELL PEPPERS (ANY COLOR)
- 1 TABLESPOON OLIVE OIL
- 1/2 CUP ONION, FINELY CHOPPED
- 2 CLOVES GARLIC, MINCED
- 1 CUP COOKED RICE OR QUINOA
- 1 POUND GROUND MEAT (BEEF, TURKEY, OR CHICKEN) OR A VEGETARIAN ALTERNATIVE LIKE CHOPPED MUSHROOMS
- 1 CUP DICED TOMATOES (CANNED OR FRESH)
- 1 TEASPOON SALT
- 1/2 TEASPOON BLACK PEPPER
- 1 TEASPOON SMOKED PAPRIKA
- 1/2 CUP SHREDDED CHEESE (CHEDDAR, MOZZARELLA, OR YOUR CHOICE)
- FRESH PARSLEY, CHOPPED (FOR GARNISH)

INSTRUCTIONS

- **PREPARE THE BELL PEPPERS:** CUT THE TOPS OFF THE BELL PEPPERS AND REMOVE THE SEEDS AND MEMBRANES. SET ASIDE THE TOPS IF YOU WISH TO USE THEM AS 'LIDS'.

- **COOK THE FILLING:** HEAT THE OLIVE OIL IN A SKILLET OVER MEDIUM HEAT. ADD THE ONION AND GARLIC, SAUTÉING UNTIL THEY ARE SOFT AND TRANSLUCENT. ADD THE GROUND MEAT OR MUSHROOMS TO THE SKILLET. COOK UNTIL BROWNED AND NO LONGER PINK. DRAIN ANY EXCESS FAT. STIR IN THE COOKED RICE OR QUINOA, DICED TOMATOES, SALT, PEPPER, AND SMOKED PAPRIKA. COOK FOR AN ADDITIONAL 5 MINUTES, ALLOWING THE FLAVORS TO MELD TOGETHER.

- **STUFF THE PEPPERS:** SPOON THE FILLING INTO EACH BELL PEPPER, PRESSING DOWN SLIGHTLY TO PACK IT IN. TOP EACH PEPPER WITH SHREDDED CHEESE.

- **GRILL THE PEPPERS:** PREHEAT THE GRILL TO MEDIUM HEAT. PLACE THE STUFFED BELL PEPPERS ON THE GRILL. IF USING THE PEPPER TOPS AS LIDS, PLACE THEM BACK ON TOP OF THE PEPPERS. COVER AND GRILL FOR ABOUT 15-20 MINUTES, OR UNTIL THE PEPPERS ARE TENDER AND THE CHEESE ON TOP IS MELTED AND BUBBLY.

- **SERVE:** CAREFULLY REMOVE THE BELL PEPPERS FROM THE GRILL. GARNISH WITH FRESH PARSLEY BEFORE SERVING.

SIDES

CLASSIC COLESLAW

SERVED: 6-8   PREP TIME: 15 MIN   TOTAL TIME: 1 HOUR 15 MIN

INGREDIENTS

- 1 MEDIUM HEAD OF GREEN CABBAGE, FINELY SHREDDED
- 2 MEDIUM CARROTS, PEELED AND GRATED
- 1/2 CUP MAYONNAISE
- 2 TABLESPOONS APPLE CIDER VINEGAR
- 1 TABLESPOON DIJON MUSTARD
- 2 TABLESPOONS SUGAR (ADJUST TO TASTE)
- 1/2 TEASPOON SALT
- 1/4 TEASPOON FRESHLY GROUND BLACK PEPPER
- OPTIONAL: 1/4 CUP FINELY CHOPPED ONION OR 1/2 CUP THINLY SLICED GREEN ONIONS FOR EXTRA FLAVOR

INSTRUCTIONS

- **PREPARE THE VEGETABLES:** USING A SHARP KNIFE, A MANDOLINE, OR A FOOD PROCESSOR WITH A SLICING ATTACHMENT, SHRED THE CABBAGE INTO FINE STRIPS. GRATE THE CARROTS USING A BOX GRATER OR THE GRATING ATTACHMENT ON A FOOD PROCESSOR.

- **MIX THE DRESSING:** IN A LARGE MIXING BOWL, WHISK TOGETHER THE MAYONNAISE, APPLE CIDER VINEGAR, DIJON MUSTARD, SUGAR, SALT, AND BLACK PEPPER UNTIL SMOOTH AND WELL COMBINED. TASTE AND ADJUST THE SEASONING OR SWEETNESS AS DESIRED.

- **COMBINE INGREDIENTS:** ADD THE SHREDDED CABBAGE AND GRATED CARROTS TO THE BOWL WITH THE DRESSING. IF USING, ALSO ADD THE CHOPPED ONION OR GREEN ONIONS. TOSS EVERYTHING TOGETHER UNTIL THE VEGETABLES ARE EVENLY COATED WITH THE DRESSING.

- **CHILL BEFORE SERVING:** COVER THE COLESLAW AND REFRIGERATE FOR AT LEAST ONE HOUR BEFORE SERVING. THIS CHILLING TIME ALLOWS THE FLAVORS TO MELD AND THE CABBAGE TO SOFTEN SLIGHTLY.

- **SERVE:** GIVE THE COLESLAW A QUICK MIX BEFORE SERVING TO REDISTRIBUTE THE DRESSING. SERVE CHILLED AS A SIDE DISH WITH GRILLED MEATS, SANDWICHES, OR AS PART OF A PICNIC SPREAD.

CHEESY GRILLED GARLIC BREAD

SERVED: 4-6　　　PREP TIME: 10 MIN　　　COOKING: 5-7 MIN　　　TOTAL TIME: 15-17 MIN

INGREDIENTS

- 1 LOAF OF FRENCH BREAD OR ITALIAN BREAD
- 1/2 CUP UNSALTED BUTTER, SOFTENED
- 4 CLOVES GARLIC, MINCED
- 1/4 CUP FRESH PARSLEY, FINELY CHOPPED
- 1 CUP SHREDDED MOZZARELLA CHEESE (OR A MIX OF YOUR FAVORITE CHEESES LIKE PARMESAN, CHEDDAR, ETC.)
- SALT AND FRESHLY GROUND BLACK PEPPER, TO TASTE
- OPTIONAL: RED PEPPER FLAKES FOR A SPICY KICK

INSTRUCTIONS

- **PREPARE THE GARLIC BUTTER:** IN A SMALL BOWL, COMBINE THE SOFTENED BUTTER, MINCED GARLIC, CHOPPED PARSLEY, AND A PINCH OF SALT AND PEPPER. MIX WELL UNTIL ALL THE INGREDIENTS ARE THOROUGHLY COMBINED.

- **PREHEAT THE GRILL:** PREHEAT YOUR GRILL TO MEDIUM HEAT. ENSURE THE GRATES ARE CLEAN TO PREVENT STICKING.

- **PREPARE THE BREAD:** SLICE THE LOAF OF BREAD IN HALF LENGTHWISE. SPREAD THE GARLIC BUTTER MIXTURE GENEROUSLY ON THE CUT SIDES OF BOTH HALVES OF THE BREAD.

- **ADD CHEESE:** SPRINKLE THE SHREDDED CHEESE EVENLY OVER THE BUTTERED BREAD. ADD RED PEPPER FLAKES IF USING.

- **GRILL THE GARLIC BREAD:** PLACE THE BREAD HALVES, CHEESE SIDE UP, ON THE GRILL. COVER THE GRILL AND COOK FOR ABOUT 5-7 MINUTES, OR UNTIL THE CHEESE IS MELTED AND BUBBLY AND THE BREAD IS NICELY TOASTED.

- **SERVE:** REMOVE THE BREAD FROM THE GRILL AND LET IT COOL FOR A FEW MINUTES. CUT THE GARLIC BREAD INTO MANAGEABLE PIECES AND SERVE WARM.

SMOKEY BABA GANOUSH

SERVED: 4-6   **PREP TIME: 10 MIN**   **COOKING: 20 MIN**   **TOTAL TIME: 50 MIN**

INGREDIENTS

- 2 LARGE EGGPLANTS
- 3 TABLESPOONS TAHINI (SESAME SEED PASTE)
- 2 CLOVES OF GARLIC, MINCED
- JUICE OF 1 LEMON
- 2 TABLESPOONS OLIVE OIL, PLUS EXTRA FOR DRIZZLING
- SALT TO TASTE
- 1/2 TEASPOON SMOKED PAPRIKA OR CUMIN (OPTIONAL, FOR ADDITIONAL SMOKINESS AND FLAVOR)
- FRESH PARSLEY, CHOPPED (FOR GARNISH)
- POMEGRANATE SEEDS (OPTIONAL, FOR GARNISH)

INSTRUCTIONS

- **GRILL THE EGGPLANT:** PREHEAT YOUR GRILL TO MEDIUM-HIGH HEAT. PRICK THE EGGPLANTS WITH A FORK SEVERAL TIMES. THIS PREVENTS THEM FROM BURSTING WHILE GRILLING DUE TO STEAM BUILDUP. PLACE THE EGGPLANTS DIRECTLY ON THE GRILL. COOK THEM, TURNING OCCASIONALLY, UNTIL THE SKINS ARE BLACKENED AND THE FLESH FEELS VERY SOFT THROUGHOUT, ABOUT 15-20 MINUTES. REMOVE THE EGGPLANTS FROM THE GRILL AND LET THEM COOL.

- **PREPARE THE EGGPLANT:** ONCE THE EGGPLANTS ARE COOL ENOUGH TO HANDLE, PEEL OFF THE CHARRED SKIN. IT SHOULD COME OFF EASILY. DISCARD THE SKIN. PLACE THE SOFT FLESH IN A COLANDER AND LET IT DRAIN FOR ABOUT 10 MINUTES TO REMOVE EXCESS MOISTURE. THIS HELPS TO CONCENTRATE THE FLAVOR AND IMPROVE THE TEXTURE.

- **MAKE THE BABA GANOUSH:** TRANSFER THE EGGPLANT FLESH TO A MIXING BOWL. ADD THE TAHINI, MINCED GARLIC, LEMON JUICE, AND OLIVE OIL. USE A FORK TO MASH THE INGREDIENTS TOGETHER UNTIL WELL COMBINED BUT STILL RETAINING SOME TEXTURE. ALTERNATIVELY, FOR A SMOOTHER TEXTURE, YOU CAN USE A FOOD PROCESSOR TO BLEND THE INGREDIENTS BRIEFLY. SEASON WITH SALT AND SMOKED PAPRIKA OR CUMIN IF USING. MIX WELL TO INCORPORATE.

- **SERVE:** TRANSFER THE BABA GANOUSH TO A SERVING DISH. CREATE A WELL IN THE CENTER AND DRIZZLE ADDITIONAL OLIVE OIL OVER THE TOP. GARNISH WITH CHOPPED PARSLEY AND, IF DESIRED, POMEGRANATE SEEDS FOR A TOUCH OF SWEETNESS AND COLOR. SERVE CHILLED OR AT ROOM TEMPERATURE WITH PITA BREAD, PITA CHIPS, OR A SELECTION OF RAW VEGETABLES FOR DIPPING.

MEXICAN STREET CORN (ELOTE)

SERVED: 4   PREP TIME: 10 MIN   COOKING: 10 MIN   TOTAL TIME: 25 MIN

INGREDIENTS

- 4 EARS OF CORN, HUSKED
- 1/4 CUP MAYONNAISE
- 1/4 CUP SOUR CREAM
- 1/2 CUP CRUMBLED COTIJA CHEESE (OR FETA CHEESE)
- 1 TEASPOON CHILI POWDER
- 1/4 TEASPOON SMOKED PAPRIKA
- 1/4 CUP CHOPPED FRESH CILANTRO (OPTIONAL)
- 1 LIME, CUT INTO WEDGES
- SALT AND PEPPER TO TASTE

INSTRUCTIONS

- <u>GRILL THE CORN:</u> PREHEAT YOUR GRILL TO MEDIUM-HIGH HEAT. PLACE THE HUSKED EARS OF CORN DIRECTLY ON THE GRILL. COOK, TURNING OCCASIONALLY, UNTIL THE CORN IS CHARRED IN SPOTS AND TENDER, ABOUT 10-15 MINUTES.

- <u>PREPARE THE SAUCE:</u> IN A SMALL BOWL, MIX TOGETHER THE MAYONNAISE, SOUR CREAM, CHILI POWDER, SMOKED PAPRIKA, SALT, AND PEPPER. ADJUST THE SEASONING TO TASTE.

- <u>COAT THE CORN:</u> ONCE THE CORN IS GRILLED, USE A BRUSH OR SPOON TO COAT EACH EAR OF CORN GENEROUSLY WITH THE CREAMY SAUCE.

- <u>TOP WITH CHEESE:</u> SPRINKLE THE CRUMBLED COTIJA CHEESE OR FETA CHEESE EVENLY OVER THE CORN, PRESSING LIGHTLY SO IT ADHERES TO THE SAUCE.

- <u>GARNISH AND SERVE:</u> TRANSFER THE COATED CORN TO A SERVING PLATTER. GARNISH WITH CHOPPED CILANTRO, IF DESIRED, AND SERVE WITH LIME WEDGES ON THE SIDE FOR SQUEEZING OVER THE CORN JUST BEFORE EATING.

ITALIAN GRILLED POLENTA

SERVED: 4-6   **PREP TIME: 20 MIN**   **COOK TIME: 10 MIN**   **TOTAL TIME: 2 HOURS 30 MIN**

INGREDIENTS

- 1 CUP POLENTA (CORNMEAL)
- 4 CUPS WATER OR VEGETABLE BROTH
- 1 TEASPOON SALT
- 2 TABLESPOONS BUTTER
- 1/2 CUP GRATED PARMESAN CHEESE
- OLIVE OIL, FOR BRUSHING
- OPTIONAL TOPPINGS: SAUTÉED MUSHROOMS, MARINARA SAUCE, OR GRILLED VEGETABLES

INSTRUCTIONS

- <u>COOK THE POLENTA:</u> IN A MEDIUM SAUCEPAN, BRING THE WATER OR VEGETABLE BROTH TO A BOIL. ADD THE SALT. GRADUALLY WHISK IN THE POLENTA TO PREVENT LUMPS. REDUCE THE HEAT TO LOW AND CONTINUE TO COOK, STIRRING FREQUENTLY, UNTIL THE POLENTA THICKENS AND STARTS TO PULL AWAY FROM THE SIDES OF THE PAN, ABOUT 15-20 MINUTES. REMOVE FROM HEAT AND STIR IN THE BUTTER AND GRATED PARMESAN CHEESE UNTIL WELL INCORPORATED.

- <u>CHILL THE POLENTA:</u> POUR THE COOKED POLENTA INTO A GREASED BAKING DISH OR TRAY, SPREADING IT OUT TO AN EVEN THICKNESS OF ABOUT 1/2 INCH. COVER AND REFRIGERATE UNTIL FIRM, ABOUT 1-2 HOURS OR OVERNIGHT.

- <u>PREPARE FOR GRILLING:</u> ONCE THE POLENTA IS FIRM, CUT IT INTO SQUARES, RECTANGLES, OR ROUNDS USING A COOKIE CUTTER. BRUSH EACH PIECE LIGHTLY WITH OLIVE OIL ON BOTH SIDES TO PREVENT STICKING TO THE GRILL.

- <u>GRILL THE POLENTA:</u> PREHEAT THE GRILL TO MEDIUM-HIGH HEAT. PLACE THE POLENTA PIECES ON THE GRILL. GRILL FOR ABOUT 4-5 MINUTES ON EACH SIDE, OR UNTIL YOU GET NICE GRILL MARKS AND THE PIECES ARE HEATED THROUGH.

- <u>SERVE:</u> SERVE THE GRILLED POLENTA WARM, TOPPED WITH YOUR CHOICE OF TOPPINGS SUCH AS SAUTÉED MUSHROOMS, MARINARA SAUCE, OR A MIX OF GRILLED VEGETABLES. GARNISH WITH ADDITIONAL PARMESAN CHEESE AND FRESH HERBS IF DESIRED.

MIDDLE EASTERN TABBOULEH

SERVED: 6-8   PREP TIME: 45 MIN   COOK TIME: 30 MIN   TOTAL TIME: 45 MIN

INGREDIENTS

- 1 CUP BULGUR WHEAT
- 1 1/2 CUPS BOILING WATER
- 3 CUPS FRESH PARSLEY, FINELY CHOPPED
- 1/2 CUP FRESH MINT LEAVES, FINELY CHOPPED
- 4 MEDIUM TOMATOES, FINELY DICED
- 1 CUCUMBER, FINELY DICED (OPTIONAL)
- 4 GREEN ONIONS, THINLY SLICED
- JUICE OF 2 LEMONS
- 1/3 CUP OLIVE OIL
- SALT AND PEPPER, TO TASTE

INSTRUCTIONS

- **PREPARE THE BULGUR:** PLACE THE BULGUR IN A LARGE BOWL. POUR THE BOILING WATER OVER IT, COVER, AND LET IT STAND FOR ABOUT 30 MINUTES, OR UNTIL THE WATER IS ABSORBED AND THE BULGUR IS TENDER. FLUFF IT WITH A FORK.

- **CHOP THE VEGETABLES:** WHILE THE BULGUR IS SOAKING, PREPARE THE VEGETABLES. FINELY CHOP THE PARSLEY AND MINT LEAVES. DICE THE TOMATOES AND CUCUMBER, AND SLICE THE GREEN ONIONS.

- **MIX THE SALAD:** IN THE BOWL WITH THE SOAKED BULGUR, ADD THE CHOPPED PARSLEY, MINT, TOMATOES, CUCUMBER, AND GREEN ONIONS. TOSS TO COMBINE.

- **DRESS THE TABBOULEH:** IN A SMALL BOWL, WHISK TOGETHER THE LEMON JUICE, OLIVE OIL, SALT, AND PEPPER. POUR THIS DRESSING OVER THE SALAD AND MIX WELL TO ENSURE EVERYTHING IS EVENLY COATED.

- **CHILL AND SERVE:** LET THE TABBOULEH CHILL IN THE REFRIGERATOR FOR AT LEAST ONE HOUR TO ALLOW THE FLAVORS TO MELD TOGETHER. THIS STEP IS CRUCIAL AS IT ENHANCES THE OVERALL TASTE. ADJUST THE SEASONING IF NECESSARY, ADDING MORE LEMON JUICE, SALT, OR OLIVE OIL ACCORDING TO YOUR PREFERENCE.

DESSERTS

GRILLED PINEAPPLE WITH CINNAMON HONEY DRIZZLE

SERVED: 4-6   PREP TIME: 10 MIN   COOK TIME: 4-6 MIN   TOTAL TIME: 16 MIN

INGREDIENTS

- 1 WHOLE PINEAPPLE
- 1/4 CUP HONEY
- 1/2 TEASPOON GROUND CINNAMON
- 2 TABLESPOONS MELTED BUTTER
- OPTIONAL: A PINCH OF GROUND CLOVES OR NUTMEG FOR EXTRA SPICE
- VANILLA ICE CREAM OR WHIPPED CREAM, FOR SERVING (OPTIONAL)

INSTRUCTIONS

- **PREPARE THE PINEAPPLE:** PEEL THE PINEAPPLE AND CUT IT INTO RINGS OR LONG WEDGES, DEPENDING ON YOUR PREFERENCE. REMOVE THE CORE IF DESIRED.

- **PREPARE THE CINNAMON HONEY DRIZZLE:** IN A SMALL BOWL, COMBINE THE HONEY AND GROUND CINNAMON (AND CLOVES OR NUTMEG IF USING). MIX WELL UNTIL FULLY BLENDED.

- **GRILL THE PINEAPPLE:** PREHEAT THE GRILL TO MEDIUM-HIGH HEAT. BRUSH EACH PINEAPPLE SLICE OR WEDGE LIGHTLY WITH MELTED BUTTER. THIS HELPS PREVENT STICKING AND ADDS A RICH FLAVOR. PLACE THE PINEAPPLE ON THE GRILL AND COOK FOR ABOUT 2-3 MINUTES ON EACH SIDE, OR UNTIL GRILL MARKS APPEAR AND THE PINEAPPLE IS SLIGHTLY SOFTENED.

- **APPLY THE HONEY DRIZZLE:** WHILE THE PINEAPPLE IS STILL WARM FROM THE GRILL, DRIZZLE IT WITH THE CINNAMON HONEY MIXTURE. THE HEAT WILL HELP THE HONEY SPREAD EASILY AND ALLOW THE FLAVORS TO MELD WITH THE PINEAPPLE.

- **SERVE:** SERVE THE GRILLED PINEAPPLE SLICES WARM. THEY CAN BE ENJOYED ON THEIR OWN OR TOPPED WITH A SCOOP OF VANILLA ICE CREAM OR A DOLLOP OF WHIPPED CREAM FOR AN ADDED TREAT.

GRILLED POUND CAKE WITH BERRY COMPOTE

SERVED: 4-6   PREP TIME: 20 MIN   COOK TIME: 15 MIN   TOTAL TIME: 37 MIN

INGREDIENTS

FOR THE GRILLED POUND CAKE:

- 1 POUND CAKE, STORE-BOUGHT OR HOMEMADE, SLICED INTO 1-INCH THICK PIECES
- BUTTER FOR BRUSHING

FOR THE BERRY COMPOTE:

- 2 CUPS MIXED BERRIES (SUCH AS STRAWBERRIES, BLUEBERRIES, RASPBERRIES, AND BLACKBERRIES)
- 1/4 CUP SUGAR
- 1 TEASPOON LEMON JUICE
- 1/2 TEASPOON VANILLA EXTRACT

INSTRUCTIONS

- **PREPARE THE BERRY COMPOTE:** IN A SAUCEPAN OVER MEDIUM HEAT, COMBINE THE MIXED BERRIES, SUGAR, AND LEMON JUICE. COOK, STIRRING OCCASIONALLY, UNTIL THE BERRIES BREAK DOWN AND THE SAUCE THICKENS, ABOUT 10-15 MINUTES. REMOVE FROM HEAT AND STIR IN THE VANILLA EXTRACT. SET ASIDE TO COOL SLIGHTLY.

- **GRILL THE POUND CAKE:** PREHEAT THE GRILL TO MEDIUM-HIGH HEAT. BRUSH BOTH SIDES OF EACH POUND CAKE SLICE LIGHTLY WITH BUTTER. PLACE THE SLICES ON THE GRILL AND COOK FOR ABOUT 1-2 MINUTES PER SIDE, OR UNTIL GOLDEN BROWN WITH GRILL MARKS.

- **SERVE:** ARRANGE THE GRILLED POUND CAKE SLICES ON PLATES. SPOON THE WARM BERRY COMPOTE OVER THE GRILLED POUND CAKE.

- **OPTIONAL:** SERVE WITH A SCOOP OF VANILLA ICE CREAM OR A DOLLOP OF WHIPPED CREAM FOR ADDED INDULGENCE.

CHOCOLATE-STUFFED FRENCH TOAST SKEWERS

SERVED: 4-6   PREP TIME: 15 MIN   COOK TIME: 4-6 MIN   TOTAL TIME: 25 MIN

INGREDIENTS

- 1 LOAF FRENCH BREAD, CUT INTO 1-INCH CUBES
- 1 CUP MILK
- 2 LARGE EGGS
- 1 TEASPOON VANILLA EXTRACT
- 2 TABLESPOONS SUGAR
- 1/2 TEASPOON CINNAMON
- 1 CUP CHOCOLATE CHIPS OR CHUNKS
- BUTTER OR OIL, FOR GRILLING
- POWDERED SUGAR, FOR SERVING
- MAPLE SYRUP OR CHOCOLATE SYRUP, FOR SERVING

INSTRUCTIONS

- <u>PREPARE THE FRENCH TOAST BATTER:</u> IN A LARGE BOWL, WHISK TOGETHER MILK, EGGS, VANILLA EXTRACT, SUGAR, AND CINNAMON.

- <u>ASSEMBLE SKEWERS:</u> SKEWER THE BREAD CUBES, INSERTING CHOCOLATE CHIPS BETWEEN THE PIECES OF BREAD.

- <u>DIP AND SOAK:</u> DIP EACH SKEWER INTO THE FRENCH TOAST BATTER, ALLOWING THE BREAD TO SOAK UP SOME OF THE MIXTURE.

- <u>GRILL:</u>
  - PREHEAT THE GRILL TO MEDIUM HEAT AND LIGHTLY GREASE WITH BUTTER OR OIL.
  - PLACE THE SKEWERS ON THE GRILL, TURNING OCCASIONALLY, UNTIL THE BREAD IS GOLDEN AND CRISP, AND THE CHOCOLATE HAS MELTED, ABOUT 2-3 MINUTES PER SIDE.

- <u>SERVE:</u> SPRINKLE WITH POWDERED SUGAR AND DRIZZLE WITH MAPLE SYRUP OR CHOCOLATE SYRUP BEFORE SERVING.

GRILLED BANANA BOATS

SERVED: 4   PREP TIME: 10 MIN   COOK TIME: 10 MIN   TOTAL TIME: 15-20 MIN

INGREDIENTS

- 4 RIPE BANANAS
- 1/2 CUP CHOCOLATE CHIPS
- 1/2 CUP MINI MARSHMALLOWS
- OPTIONAL TOPPINGS: CRUSHED GRAHAM CRACKERS, NUTS, PEANUT BUTTER, CARAMEL SAUCE, OR COCONUT FLAKES

INSTRUCTIONS

- **PREPARE THE BANANAS:** LEAVE THE PEEL ON AND SLICE EACH BANANA LENGTHWISE, MAKING SURE NOT TO CUT ALL THE WAY THROUGH TO THE OTHER SIDE. THE PEEL SHOULD ACT AS A "BOAT" TO HOLD THE INGREDIENTS.

- **STUFF THE BANANAS:** GENTLY OPEN EACH BANANA SLIGHTLY AND STUFF WITH CHOCOLATE CHIPS AND MARSHMALLOWS. FEEL FREE TO ADD ANY ADDITIONAL TOPPINGS OF YOUR CHOICE LIKE A SPOONFUL OF PEANUT BUTTER OR A SPRINKLE OF NUTS.

- **WRAP THE BANANAS:** WRAP EACH BANANA INDIVIDUALLY IN ALUMINUM FOIL, MAKING SURE THEY ARE WELL SEALED BUT WITH SPACE ON TOP TO ALLOW THE TOPPINGS TO MELT WITHOUT STICKING TO THE FOIL.

- **GRILL THE BANANAS:** PREHEAT THE GRILL TO MEDIUM-HIGH HEAT. PLACE THE FOIL-WRAPPED BANANAS ON THE GRILL AND COOK FOR ABOUT 5-10 MINUTES, OR UNTIL THE BANANAS ARE SOFT AND THE TOPPINGS HAVE MELTED.

- **SERVE:** CAREFULLY OPEN THE FOIL (WATCH FOR STEAM) AND CHECK IF THE BANANAS ARE TENDER AND THE TOPPINGS ARE GOOEY. SPRINKLE WITH CRUSHED GRAHAM CRACKERS IF DESIRED, FOR THAT CLASSIC S'MORES FLAVOR.

GRILLED PEACH AND RICOTTA PARCELS

SERVED: 4   PREP TIME: 15 MIN   COOK TIME: 15-20 MIN   TOTAL TIME: 35 MIN

INGREDIENTS

- 4 LARGE PEACHES, HALVED AND PITTED
- 1 CUP RICOTTA CHEESE
- 2 TABLESPOONS HONEY, PLUS EXTRA FOR DRIZZLING
- 1 TEASPOON VANILLA EXTRACT
- 1/4 TEASPOON GROUND CINNAMON
- ZEST OF 1 LEMON
- FRESH MINT LEAVES, FOR GARNISH
- ALUMINUM FOIL FOR WRAPPING

INSTRUCTIONS

- **PREPARE THE RICOTTA MIXTURE:** IN A BOWL, COMBINE THE RICOTTA CHEESE, HONEY, VANILLA EXTRACT, CINNAMON, AND LEMON ZEST. MIX WELL UNTIL THE INGREDIENTS ARE THOROUGHLY BLENDED AND SMOOTH.

- **STUFF THE PEACHES:** TAKE EACH PEACH HALF AND SPOON A GENEROUS AMOUNT OF THE RICOTTA MIXTURE INTO THE CAVITY WHERE THE PIT WAS REMOVED.

- **WRAP THE PEACHES:** CUT ALUMINUM FOIL INTO LARGE SQUARES THAT CAN COMFORTABLY WRAP AROUND A PEACH HALF. PLACE A STUFFED PEACH HALF, CUT SIDE UP, ON EACH SQUARE OF FOIL. BRING THE EDGES OF THE FOIL UP AND AROUND THE PEACH, TWISTING AT THE TOP TO SECURE IT INTO A PARCEL. ENSURE THE FOIL IS SEALED WELL TO KEEP THE CHEESE MIXTURE FROM LEAKING OUT DURING GRILLING.

- **GRILL THE PARCELS:** PREHEAT THE GRILL TO MEDIUM HEAT. PLACE THE FOIL PARCELS ON THE GRILL AND COOK FOR ABOUT 15-20 MINUTES, TURNING ONCE, UNTIL THE PEACHES ARE TENDER AND HEATED THROUGH.

- **SERVE:** CAREFULLY OPEN EACH FOIL PARCEL (WATCH FOR STEAM). DRIZZLE THE PEACHES WITH A LITTLE MORE HONEY IF DESIRED. GARNISH WITH FRESH MINT LEAVES FOR A REFRESHING TOUCH. SERVE WARM, RIGHT OUT OF THE FOIL FOR A RUSTIC PRESENTATION, OR TRANSFER TO PLATES IF PREFERRED.

SMOKED APPLE CRISP

SERVED: 6-8   PREP TIME: 20 MIN   TOTAL TIME: 2 HOURS 20 MIN

INGREDIENTS

FOR THE FILLING:

- 6 LARGE APPLES (SUCH AS GRANNY SMITH OR HONEYCRISP), PEELED, CORED, AND SLICED
- 1/2 CUP GRANULATED SUGAR
- 2 TABLESPOONS ALL-PURPOSE FLOUR
- 1 TEASPOON GROUND CINNAMON
- 1/2 TEASPOON GROUND NUTMEG
- JUICE OF 1 LEMON

FOR THE TOPPING:

- 3/4 CUP ALL-PURPOSE FLOUR
- 3/4 CUP OLD-FASHIONED OATS
- 3/4 CUP BROWN SUGAR
- 1/2 TEASPOON CINNAMON
- 1/4 TEASPOON SALT
- 1/2 CUP UNSALTED BUTTER, CHILLED AND CUBED

ADDITIONAL:

- WOOD CHIPS FOR SMOKING (APPLEWOOD IS IDEAL)
- VANILLA ICE CREAM OR WHIPPED CREAM, FOR SERVING

INSTRUCTIONS

- **PREPARE THE APPLE FILLING:** IN A LARGE BOWL, COMBINE THE SLICED APPLES WITH GRANULATED SUGAR, 2 TABLESPOONS OF FLOUR, 1 TEASPOON OF CINNAMON, NUTMEG, AND LEMON JUICE. TOSS UNTIL THE APPLES ARE EVENLY COATED. SET ASIDE.

- **MAKE THE CRISP TOPPING:** IN ANOTHER BOWL, MIX TOGETHER 3/4 CUP OF FLOUR, OATS, BROWN SUGAR, 1/2 TEASPOON CINNAMON, AND SALT. ADD THE CUBED BUTTER AND USE A PASTRY CUTTER OR YOUR FINGERS TO MIX UNTIL THE MIXTURE RESEMBLES COARSE CRUMBS.

- **ASSEMBLE THE APPLE CRISP:** TRANSFER THE APPLE MIXTURE TO A SUITABLE BAKING DISH THAT CAN GO IN YOUR SMOKER, SUCH AS A CAST-IRON SKILLET. EVENLY SPRINKLE THE OAT TOPPING OVER THE APPLES.

- **PREPARE THE SMOKER:** PREHEAT YOUR SMOKER TO ABOUT 250°F (120°C). SOAK WOOD CHIPS IN WATER FOR AT LEAST 30 MINUTES BEFOREHAND, THEN DRAIN AND ADD TO THE SMOKER.

- **SMOKE THE APPLE CRISP:** PLACE THE APPLE CRISP IN THE SMOKER. CLOSE THE LID AND SMOKE FOR ABOUT 1.5 TO 2 HOURS, OR UNTIL THE APPLES ARE TENDER AND THE TOPPING IS CRISP AND GOLDEN.

- **SERVE:** SERVE THE SMOKED APPLE CRISP WARM, IDEALLY WITH A SCOOP OF VANILLA ICE CREAM OR A DOLLOP OF WHIPPED CREAM ON TOP.

GRILLED HONEY-MINT FRUIT SKEWERS

SERVED: 4   PREP TIME: 15 MIN   COOK TIME: 4-6 MIN   TOTAL TIME: 50 MIN

INGREDIENTS

- ASSORTED FRUITS (SUCH AS PINEAPPLES, PEACHES, NECTARINES, AND STRAWBERRIES), CUT INTO CHUNKS
- WOODEN SKEWERS, SOAKED IN WATER FOR 30 MINUTES TO PREVENT BURNING
- 1/4 CUP HONEY
- 2 TABLESPOONS FRESH MINT, FINELY CHOPPED
- JUICE OF 1 LIME

INSTRUCTIONS

- <u>PREHEAT THE GRILL:</u> HEAT YOUR GRILL TO MEDIUM-HIGH HEAT.

- <u>PREPARE THE FRUIT SKEWERS:</u> THREAD THE FRUIT CHUNKS ONTO THE SOAKED SKEWERS, ALTERNATING THE TYPES OF FRUIT FOR VARIETY AND COLOR.

- <u>MAKE THE HONEY MINT GLAZE:</u> IN A SMALL BOWL, COMBINE THE HONEY, MINT, AND LIME JUICE. STIR UNTIL WELL MIXED.

- <u>GRILL THE SKEWERS:</u> PLACE THE FRUIT SKEWERS ON THE GRILL. GRILL EACH SIDE FOR ABOUT 2-3 MINUTES UNTIL THE FRUIT HAS GRILL MARKS AND STARTS TO CARAMELIZE.

- <u>GLAZE THE FRUIT:</u> BRUSH THE HONEY MINT GLAZE OVER THE FRUIT SKEWERS DURING THE LAST MINUTE OF GRILLING, TURNING THEM TO ENSURE EVEN COATING.

- <u>SERVE:</u> REMOVE THE SKEWERS FROM THE GRILL AND ALLOW TO COOL SLIGHTLY BEFORE SERVING. CAN BE SERVED AS IS OR WITH A SCOOP OF VANILLA ICE CREAM OR A DOLLOP OF WHIPPED CREAM FOR EXTRA INDULGENCE.

CONCLUSION

AS YOU CLOSE THIS BOOK, YOU ARE NOW ARMED WITH THE KNOWLEDGE AND TECHNIQUES TO ELEVATE YOUR BARBECUE TO NEW, INCREDIBLE HEIGHTS. EACH PAGE YOU'VE TURNED HAS BROUGHT YOU CLOSER TO MASTERY OF THE GRILL, TEACHING YOU NOT ONLY HOW TO PERFECT CLASSIC RECIPES BUT ALSO TO BOLDLY EXPERIMENT WITH CREATIVITY. WHETHER YOU'RE LOOKING TO IMPRESS GUESTS AT YOUR NEXT PARTY OR ENJOY A QUIET EVENING WITH FAMILY, THE SKILLS YOU'VE ACQUIRED HERE WILL ENSURE SUCCESS AND CULINARY DELIGHTS. REMEMBER: EVERY MEAL IS AN OPPORTUNITY TO CELEBRATE, EXPLORE, AND, MOST IMPORTANTLY, DELIGHT. SO KEEP GRILLING, KEEP EXPERIMENTING, AND CONTINUE TO ENJOY THE DELICIOUS JOURNEY OF BARBECUE.

HAPPY GRILLING!